Spice it up!
LEVI ROOTS

NATURAL VALLEY
FRUITS & VEGETABLES

CONTENTS

The Caribbean is famous for its spices. Island food is full of fragrant flavours, markets are piled high with vibrant chillies, and warm breezes and trade winds bear the scent of nutmeg and allspice. So, here's my book of easy-to-cook food using my favourite spices to bring new life to popular, everyday ingredients. There are plenty of recipes for everyone – some hot, many not – but all of them bringing the Caribbean sunshine vibe to your kitchen.

Back in the day, spices used to be as expensive as gold, kept under lock and key, and you can see why. Food can be so bland and normal. The big ingredients – the yams and potatoes – make up the bulk of what goes into the pot, but it's the small ones – the nutmeg, the pepper, the cinnamon – that create the flavours. They're the ones that do the tricks. Look how small cardamom and mustard seeds are, and yet how vivid. From small things come big wonders.

Spices make you imagine where they come from. Caribbean-style recipes and ingredients are bound to get you thinking of being there, living the outdoor life, the party life, and enjoying that laid-back attitude towards cooking.

The wonder of Caribbean food is that it's so varied. The motto of Jamaica (where I grew up) is 'Out of many, one people' because there are so many races together on the islands. All these peoples keep their own cuisine and their regional pots. There are lots of Indian people in the Caribbean and they cook traditional Indian food such as Roti Wraps with Chilli Chickpeas (*see* page 72). Then there are Chinese people; their spices influenced the Soy, Chilli and Star Anise Spiced Mackerel Fillets (*see* page 44). Different islands of the Caribbean bear different influences from the British, Spanish and French.

More and more people are seeing that there's nothing strange about Caribbean cuisine – they are already using the spices that come from the islands, and have long been cooking the other cuisines, such as Indian and French, that are part of island food. Nutmeg, cinnamon and ginger are already in their storecupboards. The famous Jamaican Scotch bonnet is just a better chilli than the one they might be using, giving another element of taste with its fruity flavour and strong heat.

When you put your mind to Caribbean cooking, it puts your vibe in a different place. You say 'I'm going to cook Caribbean tonight' and you're talking about maybe a barbecue – perhaps my Lime Jerk Chicken Drumsticks (*see* page 18) – and probably some sweet stuff. You're going to be excited because it's certainly not going to be boring. You might put on some music to get in the mood, perhaps dress up. In your mind, you are bringing that sunshine island into your front room. And it's going to be fun!

When I was growing up in Content, Jamaica, we had the hot spices – the ginger and chillies – and the flavoursome herb thyme growing wild in our garden. Nutmeg was grown locally, and someone around Content would give us some in exchange for vegetables that we had grown. Then we would go and get other spices from the spice lady or man in the market. We didn't have a spice rack;

we would use what we needed and wrap up the rest to put away and use soon. In them days, there wasn't such a thing as a fridge. Everything was pretty fresh – bought or gathered and used straightaway. And it's best, still, not to keep spices for too long, as they lose some of their power.

Nowadays, I have the spice world in pots on my kitchen shelves. My greatest pleasure is choosing them carefully for each dish. I always say that cooking is like making a piece of music. You lay out the ingredients like an orchestra or a band. The choice that you make is down to what flavours work together and what will complement the main ingredients. The music vibe is the merging and the mixing of these spices.

There are two elements you are thinking of: heat and fragrance. If we're talking about chillies – and if you want something that is 'Levi Spice' – it's best to have the Scotch bonnet. But whatever you use, you can turn the heat up or down by choosing to use the hot seeds or not. Whether you're talking about flavour or heat, when it comes to spices, the trick is knowing how to manage them. When you're mixing music, you never put too much volume on to start with – you can add a bit more later. Likewise, a spice mixture can be spoiled by adding too much of one thing. You can use two, three or four spices to make a particular combination, but start small – you need to balance them out and keep tasting as you go along. A spice like nutmeg can be very strong and take over, and chillies can overpower the other tastes. But get it right and the magic comes.

Cooking with spices is about the smells, the tastes, the look – spices such as vanilla pods and star anise are beautiful – the textures and the overall sensation. It's about cutting into a Scotch bonnet so that your eyes weep and your mouth waters with anticipation, and you know it's going to work because it's working even before it goes in the pot. You grate in some nutmeg, that wonderful aroma comes up and you know it's going to do the business.

As for preparation, one of my favourite bits of kit in the kitchen is a pestle and mortar. When I was growing up, we had a giant one that was used mainly for pounding coffee. My grandfather would make it from a tree trunk. He'd cut it 3ft high and put hot coals in the top, and it would take a lot of time to keep burning down to make a deep scoop for pounding into. The pestle was a big stick. Us kids would take our turn on it, and I grew up knowing how wonderfully it brought out the flavours of anything we'd want to crack, such as pimento seeds (allspice berries) – they come alive when you pestle-and-mortar them.

Spices are good in ground form for baking. For other cooking, you can chuck the whole seeds into the pot and release the flavour at a slower rate. But nothing beats grinding spices by hand in a pestle and mortar – that's when you really get the aromas. For instance, if you grind pimiento, smells of nutmeg, cinnamon and cloves are released that together give it its British name 'allspice'. So if you're really going to enjoy spices, get a pestle and mortar – I've got a wooden one I brought back from Jamaica, which reminds me of the coffee, or use a classic ceramic or stone one. But you don't even need this to have your fun and do the job. My granny used to put all her spicing stuff in a bit of cloth and use the rolling pin to bash it. When she opened it up, it was all done, perfect, old-style.

In my flavour palette for this book, I've also included the stronger-tasting herbs such as thyme and coriander leaves that are popular in Caribbean cooking. Spices are usually added during the cooking process, whereas herbs are more often than not introduced at the end. Coriander and mint work in a different way to spices, and you want to keep their freshness by adding them last of all. You can also use them in a wet seasoning, crushing thyme with garlic and salt in a pestle and mortar, and adding it to the pot at the start.

My kitchen is full of the good tastes you're about to discover. There are preserves and relishes such as Spiced Pickled Limes (*see* page 152), comfort food, for example my Super-sweet Hot Mash (*see* page 100), unusual combinations such as the Strawberry and Black Peppercorn Sauce that goes with White Chocolate and Vanilla Mousse (*see* page 130) and, of course, plenty of cakes, puddings and more chocolate – you've got to try my Wicked Caribbean Hot Chocolate (*see* page 132). There are some favourites from the Caribbean, such as My Caribbean Pepper Beef (*see* page 36), and then there are plenty of spiced-up versions of Brit foods – Mustardy Macaroni Cheese (*see* page 82) and Pineapple and Cinnamon Coconut Crumble with Nutmeg Coconut Custard (*see* pages 170 and 65). Other dishes are classics that are always fragrant with spice and here are given a Caribbean twist, such as my Caribbean Christmas Pudding with dried tropical fruit soaked in a whole lot of rum (*see* page 140). It's ultimately all about the ingredients and the fun you can have cooking and eating.

Nuff said. It's time to open these pages, open your pots and your taste buds, stir up your senses and spice it up, my friends!

This easy spin on roast chicken makes a perfect Sunday lunch dish. I like it with Tropical Fruit and Rice Pilaf (see page 76). All you need apart from that is a green veg or a big bowl of crisp, green salad.

Serves 4

1 orange

2 limes

4cm (1½in) piece of fresh root ginger, peeled and grated

1.5kg (3lb 5oz) chicken

salt and black pepper

5 sprigs of thyme, plus an extra sprig to garnish (optional)

250ml (9fl oz) orange juice

5 tbsp clear honey

30g (1oz) unsalted butter, melted

1 Preheat the oven to 170°C (fan)/190°C/gas mark 5. Finely grate the rind of the orange and the limes. Put into a bowl with the grated ginger and mix together. Cut the orange and limes into wedges.

2 Season the inside of the chicken with salt and pepper and rub it with half of the citrus rind and ginger mixture. Put the thyme sprigs inside the chicken together with 1–2 orange and lime wedges.

3 Add the orange juice, honey, melted butter and some salt and pepper to the remaining citrus rind and ginger mixture and mix together.

4 Put the chicken into a roasting tin into which it fits quite snugly and drizzle a little of the flavoured butter over it. Season the outside with salt and pepper. Add the rest of the orange and lime wedges to the roasting tin, scattered evenly around the bird.

5 Roast for 1 hour 20 minutes, basting the chicken every 20 minutes or so with the flavoured butter. Check to see if the chicken is cooked – pierce the thickest part of the thigh with a sharp pointed knife and the juices that run from it should be clear with no trace of pink. If they are still pink, roast for another 5 minutes, then test again. If the chicken gets too dark (the honey does make it darken), cover it with foil.

6 Leave the chicken to rest for 10 minutes then serve it with the cooking juices from the tin, garnished with a thyme sprig, if you like.

CHICKEN, CITRUS & POMEGRANATE SALAD WITH CHILLI-HONEY DRESSING

Not only is this salad as pretty as a picture, it's very healthy, with all that zingy, vitamin-loaded citrus and pomegranate. Don't add the seeds until you are about to serve, or they'll leach out their crimson juices.

Serves 8

1 tbsp olive oil

4 skinless chicken breast fillets, about 150g (5½oz) each

salt and black pepper

4 small oranges

2 ruby grapefruit

1 yellow grapefruit

1 small red onion, peeled

leaves from a generous bunch of mint

1 pomegranate, halved

For the dressing

4 tsp white wine vinegar, or to taste

4 tsp clear honey, or to taste

salt and black pepper

5 tbsp extra virgin olive oil, or to taste

1 small red chilli, deseeded and finely chopped

1 First make the dressing. Mix the vinegar, honey and salt and pepper to taste together in a shallow serving bowl. Whisk in the extra virgin olive oil with a fork and then add the chilli. Taste for the balance of vinegar to oil and sweet to sour, and adjust if necessary.

2 Heat the olive oil in a frying pan over a medium-high heat. Season the chicken breasts with salt and pepper, add to the pan and cook on each side so that they get a good colour. Reduce the heat to medium-low and cook for about 3 minutes on each side until they are done all the way through – cut into the thickest part of the chicken to check that it is white rather than pink in the middle. Set the chicken aside while you make the rest of the dish.

3 Treat all the citrus fruit in the same way. Cut a small slice off the top and bottom and set the fruit on a chopping board. Using a very sharp knife, cut off the rind and as much of the white pith as possible, working from top to bottom and all the way around each fruit. Now you can either cut out each segment of fruit by slicing down between the flesh and the membrane, or, if this seems too much like hard work, cut each piece of fruit crossways into slices. Flick out any seeds as you go along. Put into a wide, shallow bowl.

4 Cut the red onion into very fine slices. Cut the chicken into long, fairly thick slices. Add the dressing (with any juices from the cooked chicken) to the fruit. Add the chicken and onion to the citrus fruit, then roughly chop the mint and add to the bowl. Flick out the seeds from the pomegranate halves with a fork over the top of the salad just before you bring it to the table.

CHICKEN WITH NUTMEG, RUM & BAY LEAVES

Nutmeg, rum and bay are a great mix. You could add thyme if you want a little more herbiness, as it also works well here. This is a really comforting dish. Serve with buttery rice or mashed potato.

Serves 4

8 bone-in chicken thighs, with skin

salt and black pepper

½ nutmeg, freshly grated

juice of 1 lime

15g (½oz) butter

1 tbsp groundnut oil

50ml (2fl oz) light rum

300ml (½ pint) chicken stock or water, plus extra if necessary

5 bay leaves

1 Put the chicken thighs into a shallow ceramic or glass dish and add salt and pepper, nutmeg and lime juice. Cover and leave to marinate in the fridge for about an hour.

2 Heat the butter with the oil in a flameproof casserole dish or sauté pan with a lid over a medium-high heat. Add the chicken thighs and cook until golden all over (you want to get a good colour on the chicken, but not cook it through). You may need to do this in batches, depending on the size of your pan.

3 Add the rum, stock and bay leaves to the pan and bring to the boil. Immediately reduce the heat, cover and leave to simmer for 30 minutes. Remove the lid and, if the cooking juices are too thin, leave it off while the chicken cooks for another 10 minutes. If the juices have really reduced and there isn't enough liquid, add a little more stock.

4 Check to see if the chicken is cooked – pierce the thickest part with a sharp pointed knife and the juices that run from it should be clear with no trace of pink. Also check the dish for seasoning before serving.

I love the combination of allspice and black pepper in this dish. I haven't added any chilli heat as I want to let the fragrance of the spices come through. Although the allspice and peppercorns are great together, they somehow come even more to life when you add the nutmeg. Serve with rice or baked or mashed sweet potato and a green vegetable or salad.

Serves 4

1 tsp black peppercorns

1 tsp allspice berries

good fresh grating of nutmeg

½ tsp salt

8 bone-in chicken thighs, with skin

1 tbsp olive oil

1 onion, finely chopped

1 garlic clove, finely chopped

2 red peppers, cored, deseeded and cut into thick strips

400ml can coconut milk

juice of 1–2 limes

chopped fresh coriander, to garnish

1 Preheat the oven to 170°C (fan)/190°C/gas mark 5. Use a pestle and mortar (or a spice grinder) to grind the peppercorns and allspice berries together. Grate in the nutmeg and stir it into the other spices with the salt. This is your seasoning mixture.

2 Put the chicken into a bowl, add the seasoning mixture and mix together well – really rub in the spices and stir up the flavours. If you have time, cover and leave to marinate in the fridge for 30–60 minutes.

3 Heat the oil in a large flameproof casserole dish with a lid over a high heat. Add the seasoned-up chicken and cook for about 10 minutes until browned all over. Remove to a plate. Reduce the heat, add the onion and garlic and cook until softened, then add the peppers and cook for about 5 minutes until softened, stirring occasionally. Stir in the coconut milk and the juice of 1 lime.

4 Return the chicken to the casserole dish, cover and transfer to the oven. Cook for 40 minutes or until the thighs are cooked through – pierce the thickest part with a sharp pointed knife and the juices that run from it should be clear with no trace of pink. Season with the juice of the second lime to taste. Garnish with chopped coriander before serving.

These drumsticks deserve a drum roll! They make good music in your mouth. I like to cook chicken before it goes on the barbecue so that you get a nice crispy outside and the meat is good and tender inside – this is the Jamaican way.

Serves 4

12 chicken drumsticks

1 lime, halved, for squeezing over

For the jerk marinade

8cm (3¼in) piece of fresh root ginger, peeled and finely chopped

½ tbsp dried thyme leaves

½ tsp grated rind and the juice of 2 limes

1 tbsp clear honey

2 tbsp olive oil

1 tsp ground black pepper

1½ tsp ground allspice

½ red chilli (ideally Scotch bonnet), finely chopped, with or without seeds

1½ tsp salt

1 Mix all the marinade ingredients together in a shallow ceramic or glass dish.

2 Bring a large saucepan of water to the boil. Add the chicken, reduce the heat and simmer for 20 minutes. Drain and leave to cool slightly.

3 Now you need to 'juck' the chicken, as we say in Jamaica – prod it all over with the tip of a knife to open up the meat to the marinade. Add the chicken to the marinade and turn in the mixture until well coated. Cover and transfer the chicken to the fridge when cool and leave for at least an hour, but ideally a couple of hours or overnight.

4 Light a barbecue. When the flames have died down and the coals are glowing, lift the chicken out of its marinade and put on the grill. Cook for about 15 minutes, turning occasionally and basting with the marinade, until the outside is nicely brown. Alternatively, if you're cooking them in the oven, place the drumsticks about 20cm (8in) below a pre-heated grill and cook until browned, turning occasionally and basting with the marinade.

5 Squeeze juice from the lime halves over the chicken before serving.

This takes a bit of juggling - you have two pans and the barbecue going at the same time - but it's a great dish that's both sweet and hot. You can make the corn cakes and the bananas first, then keep them warm in a low oven while you quickly cook the chicken.

Serves 4

4–8 boneless, skinless chicken thighs

salt and black pepper

3 tbsp olive oil

leaves from 3 sprigs of thyme

juice of 2 limes

1½ tsp dried chilli flakes

25g (1oz) plain flour, seasoned

2 large eggs, beaten

25g (1oz) fresh white breadcrumbs

4 ripe bananas

25g (1oz) unsalted butter

2 tsp groundnut oil

For the corn cakes

75g (2¾oz) polenta

75g (2¾oz) plain flour

450g (1lb) canned or frozen sweetcorn (drained or defrosted)

4 large eggs

100ml (3½fl oz) milk

50g (1¾oz) butter, melted

6 spring onions, chopped

4 garlic cloves, sliced

2 red chillies, deseeded and chopped

groundnut oil, for frying

1 Put the chicken thighs into a shallow ceramic or glass dish and add salt and pepper, the oil, thyme, lime juice and chilli flakes. Cover and leave to marinate in the fridge for a couple of hours if you can.

2 For the corn cakes, put all the ingredients except the chillies and oil into a food processor and whizz using the pulse button until you have a slightly chunky mixture. Stir in the chillies and set aside while you prepare the bananas.

3 Put the seasoned flour, eggs and breadcrumbs on to separate plates. Peel the bananas and cut each one in half lengthways. Dip them in the seasoned flour, the eggs and finally in the breadcrumbs. Heat the butter with the oil in the frying pan over a medium-high heat, add the bananas and cook for about 4–5 minutes on each side until golden all over. Keep the bananas warm in a low oven.

4 Heat 1 tablespoon groundnut oil in a large nonstick frying pan over a medium heat and spoon 3 tablespoons of the corn batter into it to make a little pancake. Cook 3 pancakes at a time if you can. When bubbles form on the top and the pancake is set underneath, flip it over and cook on the other side until golden and set. Cook the remaining corn batter in the same way, adding a bit more oil to the pan as necessary. Put them in the oven to keep warm too.

5 Lift the chicken thighs out of their marinade. Transfer them to the hot barbecue, close to the heat source, and sear them for 3 minutes, turning halfway through the cooking time, until nicely coloured. Now move the chicken away from the direct heat (either move the rack on which it is cooking, or move it to a cooler part of the barbie) and cook for about 7 minutes more (it all depends on the heat of your barbecue) until it is done right through – pierce the thickest part of the chicken with a sharp pointed knife and the juices that run from it should be clear with no trace of pink. Serve with the corn cakes and bananas.

This is my own knockout version of a traditional African peanut stew. and it's great for all those who love both nuts and coconut. Serve it up with plain rice and greens.

Serves 6

1½ tbsp groundnut or sunflower oil

1 onion, finely chopped

1 red pepper and 1 green pepper, cored, deseeded and cut into chunks

1 carrot, peeled and diced

5 garlic cloves, crushed

2 red chillies, deseeded and chopped

4cm (1½in) piece of fresh root ginger, peeled and very finely chopped

4 plum tomatoes, roughly chopped

8 tbsp crunchy peanut butter

250ml (9fl oz) chicken stock

200ml (⅓pint) coconut cream

juice of 2 limes

½ tbsp white wine vinegar

1½ tbsp soft light brown sugar

leaves from 4 sprigs of thyme, plus leaves from 1 extra sprig to serve

salt and black pepper

8 boneless, skinless chicken thighs, cut into 4cm (1½in) chunks

2 tbsp chopped roasted peanuts, to serve

1 Heat the oil in a sauté pan over a medium heat. Add the onion, peppers and carrot and cook, stirring occasionally, until the onion and peppers are soft. Add the garlic, chillies and ginger and cook, stirring, for another 2 minutes. Add the tomatoes and cook, stirring occasionally, for about 5 minutes until they start to soften.

2 Stir in all the remaining ingredients, except the chicken and peanuts. Bring to the boil gently, stirring to help the peanut butter to amalgamate with everything else. Season to taste with salt and pepper and cook for about 10 minutes. Add the chunks of chicken and simmer for about 8 minutes until the chicken is cooked through – cut into one of the chunks to check that it is white rather than pink in the middle. Check the seasoning again. Sprinkle the extra thyme and the peanuts on top and serve.

LAMB SAUSAGES IN WRAPS WITH MY HOT LOVE-APPLE SAUCE

You can buy great spicy Middle Eastern lamb sausages - they're the best to use here - but you can use pork ones if that's all you can get. 'Love apple' is an old-fashioned term for a tomato. If you don't have time to prepare the sauce, replace it with 6 tablespoonfuls of my delicious Reggae Reggae Tomato Ketchup.

Serves 6

2 tbsp olive oil

12 spicy lamb or pork sausages

6 wraps (you can use rotis, naan bread, tortilla wraps or Arab flatbread)

2 ripe avocados

175g (6oz) baby spinach leaves

½ red onion, very finely sliced (almost wafer thin)

salt and black pepper

soured cream, to serve (optional)

For the sauce (or use my Reggae Reggae Tomato Ketchup)

1 tbsp olive oil

1 onion, finely chopped

4 garlic cloves, finely chopped

2 red chillis, deseeded and finely chopped

2 tsp ground cumin

395g can cherry tomatoes in thick juice

200ml (7fl oz) warm water

salt and black pepper

1 To make the sauce, heat the oil in a saucepan over a medium heat and cook the onion, stirring occasionally, for about 10 minutes until soft. Add the garlic, chilli and cumin and cook for another 2 minutes. Add the tomatoes and water, season with salt and pepper, and bring to the boil. Immediately turn the heat down and simmer for about 20 minutes, until the sauce has thickened. Transfer to a bowl and set aside.

2 Meanwhile, preheat the oven to 180°C (fan)/200°C/gas mark 6. Heat the oil in a frying pan, add the sausages and cook for about 8 minutes or until browned all over and cooked through. Lamb sausages don't need to be cooked for as long as pork ones, as they are usually thinner, so if you are using pork ones, cook them for a few more minutes to make sure they are cooked through.

3 While the sausages are cooking, heat the wraps in the oven. Just before the sausages are ready, halve, stone, peel and slice the avocados.

4 Put 2 sausages, cut in half lengthways if thicker pork ones, and an equal amount of the spinach, avocado and onion into each wrap. Season with salt and pepper and spoon on some of the warm love apple sauce (or my Reggae Reggae Tomato Ketchup, if you're using this). Because of the heat, this is also nice with a dollop of soured cream. Serve immediately.

This spiced-up twist on a great British classic is one for my grandchildren and all sausage fans everywhere. The peppers look great and add another flavour dimension. This is fantastic served in the traditional way with an onion gravy, or scatter with chopped coriander leaves and serve with a nice mango chutney. Merguez lamb sausages are good to use.

Serves 4

2 tbsp sunflower oil

8 meat or veggie sausages (ideally ones with chilli in them)

2 red peppers, cored, deseeded and cut into 10 slices

For the batter

125g (4½oz) plain flour

1–2 tsp chilli powder, or ½ red chilli (ideally Scotch bonnet), deseeded and finely chopped

¼ tsp freshly grated nutmeg

large pinch of salt

2 large eggs

150ml (¼ pint) milk

150ml (¼ pint) water

1 For the batter, put the flour into a large bowl and stir in the chilli, nutmeg and salt. Whisk the eggs with the milk and water. Make a well in the centre of the seasoned flour and pour in the liquid. Gradually draw the dry ingredients into the liquid to make a smooth batter, beating hard to remove any lumps. (Alternatively, you can make this in a food processor by adding all the ingredients and whizzing using the pulse button until you have a smooth batter.) Cover and leave to rest in the fridge for at least 30 minutes.

2 Preheat the oven to 200°C (fan)/220°C/gas mark 7. Heat 1 tablespoon of the oil in a frying pan over a high heat, add the sausages and cook on one side for about 5 minutes until browned. Meanwhile, put the remaining tablespoon of oil into a roasting tin (40cm × 20cm/16in × 8in is ideal) and place in the oven to get good and hot.

3 Transfer the sausages to the hot oil in the roasting tin, browned-side down. Pour the batter over the sausages, scatter the pepper pieces evenly around, skin-side up, and cook in the oven for 35–40 minutes until the batter is well risen and the sausages cooked through. Serve immediately.

28 HONEY-MUSTARD SAUSAGES

Lots of people love hot sausages to go with a drink, and this is a real party sausage – a sweet-spicy version of a classic snack. It's quick and easy to prepare, too, so you can soon get back to relaxing with your friends.

Serves 6–8, with drinks

- 24 chipolata cocktail sausages
- 2 tbsp clear honey
- 1½ tbsp grainy mustard

1 Preheat the oven to 160°C (fan)/180°C/gas mark 4. Put the sausages into a roasting tin and cook in the oven for 20 minutes.

2 While the sausages are cooking, put the honey into a saucepan and warm over a low heat to make it more liquid. Mix in the mustard.

3 Remove the sausages from the oven and roll them in the honey-mustard mixture. Return to the oven for another 10 minutes until browned and cooked through.

This may sound like a strange combination, but pork and vanilla go very well together - the vanilla emphasizes the sweetness of the pork - and coconut is good with both. It's quite a pale dish, so serve it with a colourful rice side and a green vegetable.

Serves 4

2 tbsp sunflower oil

4 pork chops, about 175g (6oz) each

salt and black pepper

2 onions, finely chopped

3 garlic cloves, finely chopped

1 green chilli, deseeded and chopped

2cm (¾in) piece of fresh root ginger, peeled and finely chopped

400ml can coconut cream

3 tsp soft light brown sugar

juice and finely grated rind of 1 lime

1 vanilla pod

2 tbsp chopped fresh coriander

1 Heat the oil in a large sauté pan over a high heat. Season the chops with salt and pepper then cook them until browned, about 2–3 minutes on each side. Remove from the pan to a plate.

2 Reduce the heat under the pan. Add the onions and cook over a low heat, stirring occasionally, until soft but not coloured. Add the garlic, chilli and ginger and cook, stirring, for 2 minutes. Stir in the coconut cream, sugar and half the lime juice. Slit the vanilla pod open lengthways with a sharp knife and scrape the little black seeds into the milk using the handle of a teaspoon or the tip of the knife. Season with salt and pepper. Heat until nearly boiling, but do not boil or the coconut cream will split.

3 Return the browned chops and any juices to the pan, spooning the cooking liquid all over them. Cook, uncovered, over a low heat for 30 minutes until cooked through and tender, basting the chops occasionally with the cooking liquid and turning them over halfway through the cooking time. Check to make sure that the pork is cooked through – it should be white rather than pink in the middle.

4 Add the lime rind and the remaining juice to the pan towards the end of the cooking time. Remove the vanilla pod and check the seasoning, then sprinkle with the coriander before serving.

PORK CHOPS WITH PINEAPPLE, MOLASSES & TAMARIND

A recipe for all the mums and dads out there, as I know how difficult it is to come up with easy midweek meals for the family. Serve with rice and spinach.

Serves 4

4 pork chops, about 200g (7oz) each

2½ tbsp molasses sugar

1½ tsp tamarind paste

2cm (¾in) piece of fresh root ginger, peeled and finely chopped

1 red chilli, deseeded and chopped

3 garlic cloves, crushed

juice of 1 lime

50ml (2fl oz) freshly squeezed orange juice

salt and black pepper

400g (14oz) prepared fresh pineapple, cut into chunks

2 red onions, peeled, each one cut into 6–8 wedges

1 Put the chops into a shallow ceramic or glass dish. Mix all the remaining ingredients together, except the pineapple and onion, and pour over the chops, turning them in the marinade to make sure they are well covered. Cover and leave to marinate in the fridge for about an hour.

2 Preheat the oven to 170°C (fan)/190°C/gas mark 5. Arrange the chops and their marinade in a shallow ovenproof dish, with the pineapple and onion wedges tucked in around them. Mix everything together with your hands, then bake for 35-40 minutes. Check to make sure that the pork is cooked through – it should be white rather than pink in the middle. Serve the chops straight from the baking dish with all the lovely cooking juices from the chops.

HOT CHOPS WITH AN ORANGE & TAMARIND GLAZE

This is a Caribbean version of sweet-and-sour, using sweet orange juice and sour tamarind. It's a great marriage of flavours that works especially well with lamb, but is also good with chicken. Just cook chicken breasts, thighs or drumsticks, until they are cooked through, then add the glaze at the end. Serve with white rice or potatoes and green vegetables or a salad.

Serves 4

1 tbsp olive oil

4 boneless lamb leg steaks, about 100g (3½oz) each

salt

fresh coriander leaves, to garnish

For the orange and tamarind glaze

1 tbsp finely grated orange rind

150ml (¼ pint) freshly squeezed orange juice

6 tsp tamarind paste

30g (1oz) light muscovado sugar

1 red chilli, finely chopped (seeds left in or removed, depending on how hot you like it)

1 First make the glaze. Mix all the ingredients together in a small saucepan and simmer over a low heat for 10-15 minutes, stirring occasionally, especially towards the end as it becomes stickier. Set aside.

2 Heat the oil in a frying pan over a high heat. Season the lamb all over with salt, add to the pan and cook for 2-3 minutes on each side, depending on whether you like it medium or well done. Pour over the glaze, stirring it into the fat and juices in the pan and rolling the lamb in it. Cook for another minute, stirring occasionally. Remove from the heat.

3 Put a lid over the pan and leave to rest for 5 minutes. Turn the meat over in the glaze again and serve with the rest of the glaze spooned over the top and garnished with coriander leaves.

STEAK WITH PEPPERCORN & THYME SAUCE

Here's my special Caribbean take on the classic French dish steak au poivre. I love the green peppercorns – they are fragrant and fresh tasting against the creamy sauce, and they also add a heat kick.

Serves 2

2 tbsp green peppercorns in brine, drained and rinsed

2 tbsp thyme leaves

1 tbsp olive oil

2 sirloin steaks, about 300g (10½oz) each

¼ tsp salt

very big splash of dark rum

200ml (⅓ pint) double cream

1 Use a pestle and mortar to roughly crush the peppercorns. Mix with the thyme leaves and half the oil. Pat the mixture on both sides of the steaks in a shallow ceramic or glass dish and then prod them all over with the tip of a knife to open up the meat to the seasoning. Cover and leave to stand at room temperature for 30 minutes.

2 Heat the remaining ½ tablespoon oil in a large frying pan over a high heat, and as it heats up, sprinkle the top of the steaks with half the salt. Add the steaks to the hot oil, salted-side down, and cook for about 1½–2 minutes on each side, depending on whether you like your steak rare or medium (if you like the meat well done, cook it for another minute on each side). Sprinkle the other side of the steaks with the remaining salt before turning them over. Remove the meat from the pan, cover and leave to rest in a warm place.

3 Add the rum to the frying pan and let it bubble away, scraping up the residue. Add the cream, stirring up all the lovely sticky meat residue on the bottom of the pan and letting it all bubble up to make a nice thick sauce. When ready to serve, pour half the sauce over each steak.

Try this lovely hot beef stew (a spin-off of a traditional 'pepperpot stew') with one of the rice dishes in the book - the Tropical Fruit and Rice Pilaf (see page 76) would be good - or with my Super-sweet Hot Mash (see page 100) or baked sweet potatoes.

Serves 6

12 allspice berries

1 tsp coriander seeds

1 tsp black peppercorns

1 tsp dried chilli flakes

1kg (2lb 4oz) braising beef, cut into 4cm (1½in) chunks

3 tbsp sunflower or groundnut oil

2 onions, finely sliced

1 red pepper and 1 green pepper, cored, deseeded and sliced

leaves from 7 sprigs of thyme, plus extra to garnish

2 bay leaves

500ml (18fl oz) beef stock

salt

chopped flat leaf parsley, to garnish

1 Use a pestle and mortar to grind all the spices together until you have a rough powder. Put the meat into a bowl and toss with the spice mix so that it is well coated. Cover and leave in the fridge for at least 2 hours, but overnight is even better.

2 Heat 1½ tablespoons of the oil in a large, heavy-based flameproof casserole dish with a lid over a high heat. Add the meat, in batches, and cook until browned all over – you need to get a good colour on it. Remove each batch to a plate and set aside.

3 Add the remaining oil to the pan, add the onions and peppers and cook over a medium heat, stirring occasionally, until soft and tinged with gold in places.

4 Return the meat to the pan, add the thyme, bay leaves and stock and season with salt. Bring to the boil, then immediately reduce to a simmer. Cover and leave to cook for about 2 hours, removing the lid for the last 30 minutes so that the cooking juices can reduce. Sprinkle with some more thyme leaves and chopped parsley before serving.

This piquant minced pork dish is as easy as pie to make, but what a lot of taste for very little effort. The Mexicans have picadillo, the Scots have mince and carrots and the Cubans have this. Perfect served with plain boiled white rice.

Serves 8

2 tbsp sunflower or groundnut oil

2 large onions, chopped

1 green pepper and 1 red pepper, cored, deseeded and chopped

1kg (2lb 4oz) minced pork

1 tbsp ground cinnamon

½ tbsp dried oregano

¼ tsp ground cloves

4 garlic cloves, chopped

2 red chillies, deseeded and chopped

salt and black pepper

75g (2¾oz) raisins

2 tbsp pimiento-stuffed green olives

400g can chopped tomatoes in thick juice

100ml (3½fl oz) chicken stock

15g (½oz) flaked almonds, toasted

1 tbsp red wine vinegar

1 Heat half the oil in a large saucepan over a medium-high heat, add the onions and peppers and cook, stirring occasionally, for about 15 minutes until soft.

2 Heat the remaining oil in a frying pan over a medium-high heat, add the minced pork and cook, breaking it up with a wooden spoon, for about 10 minutes until browned – you want to get a good colour.

3 Add the cinnamon, oregano, cloves, garlic and chillies to the onions and peppers and cook, stirring, for another 2 minutes. Add the browned pork and mix together.

4 Season with salt and pepper and add the raisins, olives, tomatoes and stock. Bring to the boil, then reduce the heat to medium. Cook, uncovered and stirring occasionally, for about 30 minutes until the liquid has evaporated. Stir in the almonds and vinegar and check the seasoning before serving.

HAM WITH A REGGAE REGGAE SAUCE & MUSCOVADO GLAZE

This ham is decorated with cloves, a spice that I love, which makes it look great when you bring it to the table. It's good served hot, but equally delicious cold. Either way, use any leftovers in sandwiches. This is made with the smallest size of gammon joint, but you can easily cook a larger one for a longer time and slightly increase the glaze quantities.

Serves 4

1kg (2lb 4oz) unsmoked gammon joint

500ml (18fl oz) ginger beer

2 bay leaves

1 onion, halved

1 celery stick, cut into 4 lengths

For the glaze

3 tsp Reggae Reggae Sauce

2 tsp dark muscovado sugar

finely grated rind of 1 orange

16 cloves

To serve

Chilli-roasted Irish Potatoes (*see* page 98)

spiced pickled limes (*see* page 152)

1 Put the ham into a saucepan in which it fits quite snugly and cover with the ginger beer, topping up with some water if necessary so that it is completely submerged. Tuck the bay leaves, onion and celery around the joint. Bring to the boil, then reduce the heat, cover and simmer gently for 1 hour 20 minutes until cooked through and tender.

2 Preheat the oven to 200°C (fan)/220°C/gas mark 7. Lift the ham out of the pan and leave to cool slightly.

3 Meanwhile, for the glaze, mix the Reggae Reggae Sauce, sugar and orange rind together. Carefully cut the rind off the ham, leaving a layer of the tasty fat. Make 4 shallow slashes across the ham, first in one direction and then in the other to create a crisscross pattern, and spread the glaze mixture over the fat. Put a clove in the middle of each diamond.

4 Put the ham into a roasting tin, adding a ladleful or so of the ginger beer cooking liquid to the tin, and bake for about 15-20 minutes until crispy brown but not burning. Serve hot in thick slices with my Chilli Roast Irish Potatoes and some spiced pickled limes.

MACKEREL WITH ORANGES, THYME, ALLSPICE & RED ONION

Mackerel is an oily fish, so it really comes alive when it's combined with citrus fruit, like the oranges used here. It's also cheap, healthy and easy to cook. A spinach and avocado salad and a rice dish are both good on the side.

Serves 4

3 red chillies, deseeded and finely chopped

12 allspice berries

12 black peppercorns

3 tsp ground cinnamon

salt

7 tbsp olive oil, plus extra for drizzling

2 oranges, peeled and cut into thick slices

3 red onions, cut into wedges

4 tsp soft light brown sugar

6 sprigs of lemon thyme

4 bay leaves

4 mackerel, gutted and cleaned

juice of ½ orange

roughly chopped flat leaf parsley, to garnish (optional)

1 Preheat the oven to 170°C (fan)/190°C/gas mark 5. Use a pestle and mortar to grind the chillies, allspice, peppercorns, cinnamon and 2 teaspoons of salt together until the whole spices are roughly ground. Add the oil and grind a little more until you have a loose paste.

2 Brush the orange slices and onion wedges with some of the spice paste (reserving the remainder for the fish) then put them into a roasting tin or ovenproof dish big enough to take the mackerel as well. Roast for 20 minutes. The onions should be quite tender by this stage.

3 Sprinkle the sugar over the oranges and onions, and add the lemon thyme sprigs and bay leaves.

4 Wash the mackerel inside and outside and pat dry with kitchen paper. Make 3 deep diagonal slashes down each side of the fish with a sharp knife. Brush the spice paste all over the fish, inside and outside, working some of the paste into the slashes.

5 Lay the mackerel on top of the oranges and onions, arranging them so that the oranges are more exposed than the onions, as you want them to get a little caramelized. Drizzle the mackerel with a little more oil and season with salt, then squeeze over the juice from the orange half. Return to the oven for another 20 minutes and then check the flesh at the thickest part of the fish with a sharp knife to see if it is cooked.

6 Serve the mackerel in the roasting tin or baking dish, garnished with roughly chopped parsley, if you like.

We are heading in an easterly direction here - towards Thailand, or even Japan. Mackerel is a great fish for strong spicing, as it has a robust flavour. This is a dish I cook when I'm on a bit of a health kick. You just need some stir-fried greens or beans on the side and a little bowl of rice.

Serves 4

4 tbsp soy sauce

2 tbsp soft dark brown sugar

2 tsp ground ginger

1 red chilli, deseeded and finely chopped

1 star anise

4 mackerel fillets, about 125g (4½oz) each

1 tbsp groundnut oil

6 spring onions, chopped

1 Put the soy sauce, sugar, ginger, chilli and star anise into a shallow dish and mix together. Add the mackerel fillets and turn in the marinade to make sure that the fish is well coated. Cover and leave to marinate at room temperature - you will only need to leave it for about 10 minutes.

2 Heat the oil in a nonstick frying pan over a medium-high heat. Lift the fillets out of the marinade, add them to the pan and cook on each side until they are cooked through - they will need about 4 minutes in total. Add any leftover marinade to the pan and let it bubble away for 1 minute more. Throw on the spring onions and serve immediately.

Here's an elegant, tender fish dish to eat on a summer's day, followed by some cool fruits. This is a different way of cooking salmon that's really easy and leaves the fish so succulent. Experiment as you like with the flavourings - the spice world is full of different combinations that would work in this dish. Serve with some boiled potatoes and a green salad.

Serves 4

200–300ml (⅓–½ pint) sunflower or rapeseed oil

½ Scotch bonnet chilli, finely chopped, with seeds

grated rind of 1 lime

1½ tbsp salt

2 bay leaves

4 salmon fillets, with skin, about 150g (5½oz) each

1 Put all the ingredients, except the salmon fillets, into a small saucepan. Add the salmon fillets, skin-side down, and bring slowly just to the boil. Immediately turn the heat off and cover the pan. Leave for 3 minutes.

2 Turn the salmon fillets over and bring to the boil again. Turn the heat off, cover and leave for 2 minutes.

3 Lift the salmon fillets out of the oil on to kitchen paper and pat with another piece of kitchen paper to absorb some of the surface oil. Serve warm or cold.

This is a take on traditional seasoned rice that uses a Jamaican way of cooking known as 'brown down'. With this technique, you fry your main ingredient - in this case the fish - in caramel to give it a lovely taste and colour. It's a good one-pot dish that's filling, robust and delicious.

Serves 4

300g (10½oz) white long-grain rice

3 tbsp sunflower oil

2 tbsp granulated sugar

4 salmon fillets, with skin, about 150g (5½oz) each

juice of 2 limes

700ml (1¼ pints) water

4 spring onions, green parts only, finely sliced

¼ hot red chilli (ideally Scotch bonnet), deseeded and finely chopped

½ tbsp thyme leaves

salt and black pepper

lime wedges, to serve

1 Put the rice into a sieve and rinse in cold water until the water runs clear, then drain.

2 Put the oil into a large saucepan with a tight-fitting lid and sprinkle in the sugar. Gently heat until the sugar has dissolved in the oil and is starting to brown. You can gently pull the tip of a wooden spoon across the base of the pan to encourage the dissolving, but do not stir.

3 When it is ready, increase the heat to medium, add the salmon, skin-side up, cover and cook for 3 minutes. Turn the fish over - carefully, as the caramel will be spluttering. Add the lime juice and quickly stir it into the caramel mixture, then immediately cover. Cook the salmon for another 2 minutes.

4 Check that the salmon is cooked then remove it from the pan. Add the rice to the caramel, stir it around and then add the water, spring onion greens, chilli and thyme. Season with a large pinch of salt and a very good grinding of pepper. Cover and cook over a low heat for 10–15 minutes.

5 Turn the heat off and leave to stand, covered, for another 10 minutes. Fluff the rice up with a fork and transfer to a large serving dish. Lay the salmon fillets on top and serve with lime wedges.

RUM, CHILLI & BROWN SUGAR CURED SALMON

I'm going a bit Scandinavian here, as this is really a Caribbean version of gravadlax, which is traditionally raw salmon cured in a mixture of salt, sugar and dill. It's quite a thrill to cure something of your own and this makes a great party dish.

Serves 4

1kg (2lb 4oz) piece of salmon in 2 halves (preferably organic), filleted but skin left on

6 tbsp dark rum

75g (2¾oz) soft dark brown sugar

2 red chillies, deseeded and shredded

½ tbsp coriander seeds, crushed

50g (1¾oz) sea salt flakes

3 tsp black pepper

4 tbsp chopped fresh coriander

To serve

toasted slices of wholegrain bread

Mango and Cucumber Relish (*see* page 166), optional

1 Run your hand over the salmon flesh to make sure there are no little bones in it. If you find any, remove with a pair of tweezers.

2 Spread out a piece of foil that is big enough to wrap round the salmon. Drizzle rum all over the 2 pieces of salmon and then lay one piece on the foil, skin-side down. Pour a little more rum over the fleshy side of the salmon.

3 Mix the sugar, chillies, coriander seeds, salt flakes, pepper and fresh coriander together, then press the spice and herb mix on top of the salmon flesh. Sprinkle with a little rum. Put the other piece of salmon on top, skin-side up, and sprinkle with the remaining rum.

4 Fold the foil round the salmon to make a sealed package and stand it on a grill rack set over a platter or roasting tin to catch the liquid as it leaches out of the salmon. Place a weight – like a chopping board – on top and leave in the fridge for 1–6 days, turning the package over occasionally. It is best to leave it for at least 2 days before eating it, as the flavour improves.

5 Unwrap the package and scrape the spice and herb mix off the salmon. Using a very sharp knife, cut the salmon flesh horizontally into thin slices, leaving the skin behind. Serve with toasted slices of wholegrain bread, and my Mango and Cucumber Relish, if you like.

In Jamaica you eat ackee (the national fruit) and saltfish for breakfast, and it really sets you up for the day. This recipe doesn't have ackee, but these zingy fishcakes will give you a morning boost, and they're also good for a bright-and-light lunch or supper dish.

Makes 4

200g (7oz) floury potatoes (such as King Edwards), peeled and cut into large chunks

500g (1lb 2oz) skinless white fish fillet, such as cod, haddock or pollock

50g (1¾oz) dry breadcrumbs

1 red chilli, deseeded and finely chopped

3 tbsp finely chopped fresh coriander

3 spring onions, green parts only, finely chopped

2.5cm (1in) piece of fresh root ginger, peeled and grated

½ garlic clove, finely chopped (optional)

finely grated rind of 1½ limes

salt

1 large egg, beaten

2 tbsp lime juice

1–2 tbsp olive oil

To serve

4 lime wedges

mixed leaf salad (optional)

1 Put the potato chunks into a saucepan of water and bring to the boil, then reduce the heat and simmer for about 10 minutes or until tender. Drain well.

2 If you have a steamer, steam the fish in it above the simmering water of the potatoes – the fish is cooked when the flesh just flakes when tested with the tip of a knife. Otherwise, while the potatoes are cooking, poach the fish in a saucepan of gently simmering water or milk for about 5 minutes (or cook in a microwave). Leave the fish to cool slightly, and when cool enough to handle, check it for bones and break into rough flakes. Put the breadcrumbs on a plate.

3 Mash the potatoes and then mix with the chilli, coriander, spring onion greens, ginger, garlic (if using), lime rind and 1 teaspoon salt. Add the beaten egg to the mixture to bind it.

4 Pour the lime juice over the flaked fish, then sprinkle on a little salt and gently stir it around with your fingers to season the fish well.

5 Gently stir the flaked fish into the potato mixture. Form into 4 fishcakes, about 4–5cm (1½–2in) thick. Pat them on both sides with the breadcrumbs, then put on a clean plate, cover loosely and leave in the fridge for 30 minutes to firm up a little.

6 Heat the oil in a frying pan over a medium-low heat. Add the fishcakes and cook for about 3 minutes on each side until the outside is nicely brown and they are hot all the way through. Serve with lime wedges and, if having them for lunch or supper, a salad.

This is another of the fish and rice dishes that I so love. You don't have to use white fish here - it's also very good with mackerel fillets, or even salmon. An avocado salad is nice on the side.

Serves 6

350g (12oz) white long-grain rice

700g (1lb 9oz) white fish fillets, such as cod, haddock or pollock, skin removed

12 allspice berries

10 black peppercorns

2 tsp cumin seeds

3 tbsp olive oil

1 large onion, roughly chopped

1 red pepper and 1 green pepper, cored, deseeded and chopped

3 garlic cloves, finely chopped

2 red chillies, deseeded and finely chopped

500g (1lb 2oz) tomatoes, chopped

400ml (14fl oz) light chicken or fish stock

200ml (⅓ pint) coconut milk

salt and black pepper

1 tbsp chopped flat leaf parsley

1 tbsp chopped fresh coriander

lime wedges, to serve

1 Put the rice into a sieve and rinse in cold water until the water runs clear, then drain and set aside.

2 Cut the fish into chunks about 5cm (2in) in size. Use a pestle and mortar to grind all the spices together. Rub the spice mix over the fish and set aside while you make the rest of the dish.

3 Heat the oil in a saucepan with a tight-fitting lid over a medium heat, add the onion and peppers and cook, stirring occasionally, until soft and tinged with gold in places. Add the garlic and chillies and cook, stirring, for 2 minutes. Add the tomatoes and cook, stirring occasionally, for about 4 minutes until softened. Add the rice and stir until it is well coated in the mixture. Finally, add the stock and coconut milk and season really well with salt and pepper. Bring to the boil, then immediately reduce the heat to low, cover and cook for about 15 minutes.

4 Add the fish and its spice seasoning – just nestle the chunks of fish in the rice. Cover and cook for another 5 minutes or so, then remove the lid and cook for a further 5 minutes or until the fish is cooked, the rice is tender and the liquid has been absorbed. Do not worry if you still have some juice left by the time the rice is cooked – it is also nice a bit 'soupy'. Garnish with the parsley and coriander and serve with lime wedges.

This is a good way to treat squid, and it's also a very economical dish, as squid and beans are both so cheap. It's very quick to make, too. Your fishmonger will be able to clean the squid for you.

Serves 4

4 tbsp olive oil

1 large onion, chopped

3 red chillies, deseeded and chopped

3 garlic cloves, crushed

8 allspice berries, crushed

½ tsp cumin seeds

½ tsp ground coriander

8 large plum tomatoes, quartered

salt and black pepper

500ml (18fl oz) chicken or fish stock or water

1 tbsp soft dark brown sugar

400g can black beans, drained

900g (2lb) cleaned squid, sliced

juice of 1 lemon

2 tbsp roughly chopped flat leaf parsley or coriander

boiled white rice, to serve

1 Heat half the oil in a large saucepan over a medium heat, add the onion and cook, stirring occasionally, until soft and golden. Add the chillies, garlic, allspice, cumin and coriander and cook, stirring, for another minute. Add the tomatoes, season with salt and pepper and cook for a further 3 minutes. Add the stock or water, sugar and beans, and bring to the boil. Reduce the heat and simmer gently for 15 minutes.

2 Heat the remaining oil in a frying pan over a high heat. Cook the squid in batches, stirring constantly, for 1 minute per batch. Season with salt and pepper, squeeze over a little lemon juice and add each batch of squid to the stew as it is cooked. You will need to add a little more oil to the pan each time you cook further batches of squid.

3 Stir the stew and add another good squeeze of lemon juice. Check the seasoning and add the chopped herbs before serving with boiled white rice.

Garlic and prawns is a classic European combination that takes well to a Caribbean treatment by adding chilli (especially Scotch bonnet) and using lime and fresh coriander instead of lemon and parsley. Serve with rice instead of the toasted bread for a more substantial dish.

Serves 2 as a main course or
4 as a starter

20g (¾oz) butter

1 tbsp olive oil, plus extra for drizzling

2 garlic cloves, finely chopped

400g (14oz) raw tiger prawns

¼ Scotch bonnet chilli, deseeded and very finely chopped

salt

juice of 1 lime

2–3 tbsp chopped fresh coriander

4 slices of French bread

2 limes, halved

1 Preheat a ridged griddle pan over a high heat, or the grill to high. While it heats up, heat the butter with the oil in a frying pan over a medium-low heat. Increase the heat slightly, add the garlic and let it sizzle away for a minute or so, stirring occasionally.

2 Add the prawns and chilli to the frying pan and cook, stirring, for 2–3 minutes until pink. Season with a little salt, squeeze over the lime juice and scatter with the chopped coriander.

3 Meanwhile, drizzle the French bread with a little olive oil and toast it in the ridged griddle pan or under the grill. At the last minute, add the lime halves to the griddle pan or grill rack to slightly blacken. Serve the prawns with the toasted bread and lime halves.

Wow, this is good - a great combination of flavours. If you can get your head around preparing the mussels, it's actually a very easy dish to put together and quick, too. Serve either on its own or with boiled white rice on the side.

Serves 6

1 tbsp groundnut or sunflower oil

2 onions, finely chopped

1 red pepper and 1 green pepper, cored, deseeded and chopped

5 garlic cloves, finely sliced

1 tsp ground ginger

2 tsp curry powder

750g (1lb 10oz) sweet potato, peeled and cut into 4cm (1½in) chunks

2 × 250ml cartons coconut cream

850ml (1½ pints) chicken or vegetable stock

1kg (2lb 4oz) live mussels

150ml (¼ pint) water

salt and black pepper

2 tbsp chopped fresh coriander

1 Heat the oil in a large saucepan over a medium heat, add the onions and peppers and cook, stirring occasionally, until soft and slightly coloured.

2 Add the garlic, ginger and curry powder and cook, stirring, for 2 minutes. Add the sweet potato, coconut cream and stock and bring to just under the boil. Reduce the heat to medium and leave to simmer gently.

3 Prepare the mussels. Wash them really well in a sink full of cold water. Scrub the shells, especially around the barnacles, as they can be full of sand, and pull off any stringy 'beards'. As you wash the mussels, tap each one on the side of the sink. If the mussel closes, keep it, but if it remains open, chuck it away. Discard any with damaged shells.

4 Rinse the good mussels in cold water, drain and put them into a large saucepan with the measured water. Set over a medium heat, cover and cook, shaking the pan occasionally, for about 5 minutes until the mussels have opened. Strain the mussels, reserving the cooking liquid. Pour the liquid through a sieve lined with muslin, to sieve out any remaining sand. Taste the cooking liquid - if it does not taste too salty, add it to the curry.

5 Go through the mussels and chuck away any that have not opened while they were cooking. Add to the curry, stir everything together and season with salt and pepper. Simmer until the mussels are heated through - the sweet potato should be completely soft by now. Stir in the coriander and serve immediately.

04

This is my take on the classic Mexican breakfast dish. You could also add a rasher of bacon to make it a Brit-Mex version of the all-day breakfast. As for the eggs, guess what – I like mine sunny-side up!

Serves 4

4 soft corn tortillas

400g can refried beans

1 tbsp olive oil

4 large eggs

cayenne pepper, to garnish

For the salsa

1 avocado, stoned, peeled and cut into small cubes

good squeeze of lime juice

1 tbsp olive oil

3 spring onions, chopped

½ hot red chilli (ideally Scotch bonnet), deseeded and finely sliced

4 tomatoes, roughly chopped

4 tbsp chopped fresh coriander

salt

1 Preheat the oven to 160°C (fan)/180°C/gas mark 4. Wrap the tortillas in foil and leave them in the oven to heat through while you prepare the rest of the dish.

2 For the salsa, toss the avocado with the lime juice in a ceramic or glass bowl. Heat the oil in a frying pan over a medium heat, add the spring onions and chilli and cook, stirring occasionally, for 2 minutes until lightly softened. Add the tomatoes and cook just for a minute, to give them a little warmth. Add to the avocado with the coriander and season with salt.

3 Put the refried beans into a saucepan over a gentle heat and heat through, stirring frequently to stop them sticking to the bottom.

4 Meanwhile, heat the oil in the frying pan, add the eggs and fry to your liking.

5 Lay each warm tortilla on a serving plate and spread with the refried beans. Add a fried egg to the centre of each and spoon the salsa around the outside. Sprinkle each egg with a pinch of cayenne pepper to garnish and serve immediately.

OK, I won't pretend. These aren't easy to make – they take a bit of time and care – but they are beautilicious. You need the fat you get in sausagemeat for these to work, so don't be tempted to substitute it for plain minced pork. You could also serve them with a hot relish or curry-flavoured mayonnaise.

Makes 8

10 large eggs

500g (1lb 2oz) pork sausagemeat

leaves from 6 sprigs of thyme

½ tsp freshly grated nutmeg

½ tsp ground allspice

1 tsp dried chilli flakes

salt and black pepper

50g (1¾oz) plain flour, plus extra for dusting

150g (5½oz) dry white breadcrumbs

50ml (2fl oz) milk

groundnut oil, for deep-frying

mango chutney, to serve

1 Put 8 of the eggs into a large saucepan of cold water and place over a high heat. As soon as the water starts to simmer, cook for 6 minutes. Transfer them immediately to cold water.

2 Put the sausagemeat into a bowl and add the thyme, spices and salt and pepper. Mix really well. On a lightly floured surface, press the pork out so that it is about as thin as pastry. Transfer to a large floured baking sheet, cover and leave to chill in the fridge for 30 minutes.

3 Once the boiled eggs are cool enough to handle, remove the shells. Put the flour on a plate and season with salt and pepper. Put the breadcrumbs on a separate plate. Beat the 2 remaining eggs with the milk in a bowl. Roll each egg in the seasoned flour, to encourage the sausagemeat to stick. Cut a square of the sausagemeat (just as you would do with pastry) and gently but firmly shape it round one of the eggs, making sure there are no little gaps. You can add more sausagemeat to cover it completely, but keep to the same thickness all the way round the egg. Roll the sausagemeat-covered eggs in the flour.

4 Dip each egg in the beaten egg, then roll it in the breadcrumbs. You need to take care to cover the whole egg and to gently shake off the excess breadcrumbs at each stage.

5 Put enough oil for deep-frying into a large saucepan to cover 2 of the eggs at a time. Heat the oil to 180°C/350°F (check with a deep-frying thermometer). Using a slotted spoon, lower 2 eggs into the oil. Keep your oil at a constant temperature by adjusting the heat. Cook the eggs, turning them twice, for 3 minutes until they are dark brown. Remove them from the oil as they cook and transfer them immediately to kitchen paper. Keep the cooked eggs warm in a low oven while you cook the others. Serve with mango chutney.

I like this for weekend brunch. It has Italian flavours, but I've given it the Caribbean heat treatment! This is a good dish for veggie friends, although you can serve sausages or bacon on the side for the carnivores.

Serves 4

350g (12oz) spinach, washed and any coarse stalks removed

3 tbsp olive oil

175g (6oz) pumpkin or butternut squash (prepared weight), peeled, deseeded and cut into 1.5cm (⅝in) chunks

1 large onion, roughly chopped

2 garlic cloves, finely chopped

3 red chillies (use 4 if you're brave!), deseeded and sliced

8 large eggs, lightly beaten and seasoned with salt and black pepper

175g (6oz) ricotta cheese, broken into chunks

100g (3½oz) mature Cheddar cheese, grated

salt and black pepper

1 Put the spinach into a saucepan with the water left clinging to the leaves after washing. Cover and cook over a low heat for about 4 minutes or until it has completely wilted. Leave to cool, then squeeze all the water out with your hands, roughly chop and set aside.

2 Heat 1½ tablespoons of the olive oil in a large frying pan over a medium heat. Add the pumpkin and cook, stirring occasionally, for about 10 minutes until golden and tender. Remove from the pan and put into a bowl.

3 Add the onion to the pan and cook over a medium heat, stirring occasionally, for about 7 minutes until soft. Add the garlic and chillies and cook, stirring, for another 2 minutes. Add the chopped spinach and cook it gently to drive off any moisture. Tip the vegetable mixture into the bowl with the pumpkin, mix together and set aside.

4 Preheat the oven to 180°C (fan)/200°C/gas mark 6. Heat the remaining 1½ tablespoons oil in a large frying pan that can go into the oven. Add the eggs and cook over a low heat for about 7 minutes until just set. Dot the vegetable mixture over the eggs and add the ricotta and Cheddar. Season with salt and pepper. Cook for another 4 minutes, then transfer the pan to the oven and cook for a further 10 minutes or until the egg mixture is set and the top is pale gold. Either slide out on to a warm serving plate or serve from the frying pan.

Custard is just one of those really comforting foods, and this version is extra special, with coconut milk and nutmeg added to the mix. It's fab with crumble of any kind - try it with my Pineapple and Cinnamon Coconut Crumble (see page 170).

Serves 6–8

200ml (⅓ pint) milk

200ml (⅓ pint) coconut milk

½ tsp freshly grated nutmeg

1 tsp vanilla extract

4 large egg yolks

3–4 tbsp light muscovado sugar

1 tsp cornflour

1 Reserve 1 tablespoon of the milk and put the remainder with the coconut milk, nutmeg and vanilla into a saucepan. Bring almost to the boil and then turn the heat off.

2 As the milk mixture is heating – but take care that the mixture does not boil over – whisk the egg yolks with the sugar in a heatproof bowl. Mix the reserved tablespoon of milk with the cornflour and stir into the egg yolk mixture.

3 Pour the hot milk mixture on to the egg yolk mixture, stirring as you go. Return to the pan and cook, stirring constantly, over a medium–low heat until it noticeably thickens. Serve hot or cold.

If you're a fan of set custards, then you'll love this sweet-spiced take on a French classic, flavoured with nutmeg and cinnamon in addition to the usual vanilla. You'll need four 200ml (1/3 pint) ramekins, or the same-sized metal pudding moulds. Serve with cream, if you like.

Serves 4

500ml (18fl oz) milk

½ vanilla pod

½ tsp freshly grated nutmeg

8cm (3¼in) piece of cinnamon stick, broken in half

100g (3½oz) granulated sugar

7 tbsp water

2 large eggs

2 large egg yolks

2 tbsp caster sugar

1 Pour the milk into a saucepan. Slit the vanilla pod open lengthways with a sharp knife and scrape the little black seeds into the milk using the handle of a teaspoon or the tip of the knife. Add the scraped-out pod to the milk too. Add the nutmeg and cinnamon pieces to the pan and give it all a stir. Bring to the boil, turn the heat off, cover and leave to infuse for 30–60 minutes.

2 Preheat the oven to 130°C (fan)/150°C/gas mark 2. Put the granulated sugar into a separate saucepan with 5 tablespoons of the water. Set over a low heat until the sugar has melted, then increase the heat and boil rapidly until you get a nice dark caramel. Add the remaining 2 tablespoons water and stir in. Remove from the heat and pour into 4 × 200ml (1/3 pint) ramekins – careful, it's very hot! Swirl the caramel around to coat the bottom of each ramekin.

3 Beat the whole eggs and egg yolks with the caster sugar in a heatproof bowl. Remove the vanilla pod and cinnamon pieces from the milk and bring just to the boil again. Leave to cool slightly and then pour the infused milk into the eggs, stirring as you do so. Stand the ramekins in a deep roasting tin. Divide the egg mixture between the ramekins and then pour boiling water into the roasting tin so that it comes halfway up the sides of the ramekins.

4 Bake in the oven for 1 hour or until set. Leave to cool and then refrigerate until you are ready to serve. Carefully slide a knife around the edge of each ramekin to loosen the custard and briefly dip the base of the ramekin into a bowl of hot water. Put a plate on top of the ramekin and turn both over together to unmould each crème caramel.

Here's a hot veggie dish, for all those fire lovers. Chilli's the word here, even though I've taken the seeds out of the Scotch bonnet - the beast has been tamed, but it's still wild!

Serves 4

1 tbsp olive oil

1 onion, finely chopped

1 carrot, roughly diced

2 garlic cloves, finely chopped

2 celery sticks, sliced

1 heaped tsp ground cumin

½ tsp ground allspice

1 red pepper, cored, deseeded and cut into small chunks

1 yellow pepper, cored, deseeded and cut into small chunks

300g (10½oz) button mushrooms, quartered

2 × 400g cans chopped tomatoes

1 hot red chilli (ideally Scotch bonnet), deseeded and finely chopped

2 × 400g cans red kidney beans, drained and rinsed

1 tbsp Reggae Reggae Tomato Ketchup

½ tsp soft dark brown sugar, or to taste

1–2 tsp soy sauce, or to taste

boiled white long-grain rice, to serve

1 Heat the oil in a large saucepan over a medium-low heat. Add the onion, carrot, garlic and celery and cook, stirring occasionally, until softened.

2 Add the cumin and allspice and cook, stirring, for 2 minutes. Add the peppers and cook for 2 minutes until softened, then add the mushrooms and cook for another 2 minutes, stirring occasionally. Add the tomatoes, chilli and kidney beans and give it all a good stir. Finally, add the Reggae Reggae Tomato Ketchup and sugar.

3 Cover and cook over a gentle heat, stirring occasionally, for 30 minutes. Season to taste with the soy sauce and add a little more sugar if necessary. Serve with rice.

Rotis are typical of Trinidad and the Indian community there. If you like, let the chickpeas catch on the bottom of the pan to get what Jamaican people call 'bun-bun' (or 'burn-burn'). That's when you have 'favourites time' in the kitchen - who gets the most bun-bun?

Serves 4

4 tbsp olive oil

1 onion, finely chopped

5cm (2in) piece of fresh root ginger, peeled and finely chopped

300g (10½oz) cooked chickpeas (or about 1¼ × 410g can, drained and rinsed)

3 spring onions, chopped

1 tsp dried chilli flakes

2 tsp black mustard seeds

4 tomatoes, roughly chopped

salt and black pepper

4 rotis

To serve

4 tbsp Greek yogurt

4 tsp chutney (mango or apricot) or Reggae Reggae Tomato Ketchup

1 tbsp chopped fresh coriander (optional)

1 Heat 2 tablespoons of the oil in a frying pan, add the onion and ginger and cook over a low heat, stirring occasionally, until soft.

2 Meanwhile, put the remaining 2 tablespoons oil and the chickpeas into a food processor and whizz to a rough (not smooth) paste.

3 Add the spring onions to the frying pan and cook over a medium heat, stirring occasionally, for 2 minutes until soft. Add the chilli flakes and mustard seeds and cook, stirring, for another minute, then add the tomatoes. Let it all cook together for about 5 minutes, stirring occasionally, then stir in the chickpea paste. Season with salt and pepper and cook for a further 5-10 minutes until all the flavours are combined. Taste and season again, if necessary.

4 Warm the rotis one at a time in a dry frying pan over a medium heat, turning once, until they are floppy and easy to roll.

5 To serve, put the rotis on a work surface and spoon the chickpea mixture into the centre. Dollop the yogurt and the chutney or Reggae Reggae Tomato Ketchup on top, and sprinkle over the chopped coriander (if using). Roll up the rotis and cut in half on the diagonal. Magic!

If you can't find large chillies for this, use romano peppers – the long ones – instead and add more spice to the rice. This is a very special rice dish and is best served alongside something uncomplicated. Otherwise, try it just with an avocado salad, salsa or some soured cream on the side.

Serves 4

4 long chillies (such as green Turkish ones, but make sure the variety you use isn't too hot)

sunflower oil, for brushing and pan-frying

1 onion, finely chopped

2 celery sticks, sliced

3 garlic cloves, finely chopped

1 red chilli, deseeded and finely sliced

1 green chilli, deseeded and finely sliced

300g (10½oz) brown rice and wild rice, mixed

800ml (scant 1½ pints) chicken or vegetable stock

1 bay leaf

salt and black pepper

15g (½oz) butter

200g (7oz) canned, drained or frozen sweetcorn, defrosted if frozen

8 spring onions, sliced

1 Preheat the oven to 160°C (fan)/180°C/gas mark 4. Leave the long chillies whole but prick them with the tip of a small sharp knife to prevent them exploding in the oven. Brush them with oil. Set them in a small roasting tin and cook them in the oven for about 30 minutes or until completely soft.

2 Meanwhile, heat ½ tablespoon oil in a saucepan over a medium heat. Add the onion and celery and cook, stirring occasionally, until soft but not coloured. Add the garlic and chillies and cook, stirring, for 2 minutes. Stir in the rice, cover with the stock and add the bay leaf. Bring to the boil and season with salt and pepper, then reduce the heat to a simmer. Cook, uncovered, for about 30 minutes until all the stock has been absorbed and the rice is tender. If it gets too dry, add a little water.

3 Heat the butter in a frying pan over a high heat until it is as hot as you dare without burning it. Add the sweetcorn and cook, stirring, until the butter is brown, then quickly toss in the spring onions. Add the contents of the pan to the rice and fork through. Lay the roasted chillies on top and serve immediately.

Sweet and gingery, this rice is lovely! Don't leave out rinsing the rice to remove some of the starch – that's the way rice is always prepared in the Caribbean. Serve it with spiced roast chicken or lamb.

Serves 6

300g (10½oz) white long-grain rice (ideally basmati)

25g (1oz) butter

1 onion, finely chopped

2 garlic cloves, finely chopped

1½ tsp ground ginger

100g (3½oz) dried mixed tropical fruit

25g (1oz) unsalted pistachio nuts or blanched almonds, chopped

700ml (1¼ pints) chicken stock or water

juice of 1 orange

3 sprigs of thyme

3 bay leaves

1 Put the rice into a sieve and rinse in cold water until the water runs clear, then drain.

2 Heat the butter in a heavy-based saucepan with a tight-fitting lid over a medium heat, add the onion and cook, stirring occasionally, until soft and pale gold. Add the garlic and ground ginger and cook, stirring, for 2 minutes.

3 Add the rice to the pan and cook, stirring around until the rice is well coated in the butter and just beginning to toast. Add all the remaining ingredients, bring to the boil and boil hard until you see little holes appearing in the rice, then immediately reduce the heat to very low and cover. Leave to cook for about 15 minutes until tender, without stirring, or you will release the starch and the rice will become sticky. You will need to carefully check that the rice is not burning on the bottom of the pan. Serve immediately.

I love rice cooked in coconut milk – it's so sweet. The addition of meat makes it a complete meal rather than a side dish. Beef, pork or chicken can be used instead of the lamb.

Serves 4

½ tsp dried thyme

½ tsp ground allspice

salt and black pepper

5 garlic cloves, finely chopped

juice of 1 lime

300g (10½oz) lamb neck fillet, cut into 3cm (1¼in) chunks

200g (7oz) white long-grain rice

3 tbsp groundnut oil

1 large onion, roughly chopped

1 red pepper, cored, deseeded and chopped

1 green pepper, cored, deseeded and chopped

1 cinnamon stick

½ tsp ground ginger

400ml (14fl oz) light chicken or lamb stock

200ml (⅓ pint) coconut milk

1 Scotch bonnet chilli, in perfect condition

1 tbsp chopped fresh coriander

1 tbsp chopped mint

1 Mix the thyme, allspice, 2 teaspoons pepper, just under half the garlic, and lime juice together in a ceramic or glass bowl. Add the lamb and toss with the marinade until well coated. Cover and leave to marinate in the fridge for 30 minutes, but ideally 2 hours, if you have the time.

2 Put the rice into a sieve and rinse in cold water until it runs clear, then drain.

3 Heat 2 tablespoons of the oil in a heavy-based saucepan with a tight-fitting lid over a medium heat. Add the onion and peppers and cook, stirring occasionally, until soft and tinged with gold. Add the remaining garlic, cinnamon stick and ginger and cook, stirring, for 2 minutes.

4 Add the rice and stir it around until well coated in the oil and vegetable mix. Pour over the stock and coconut milk, season really well with salt and pepper and tuck in the whole Scotch bonnet. Bring to the boil and boil hard until you see little holes appearing in the rice, then immediately reduce the heat to low and cover. Leave to cook for 15–20 minutes until just tender, without stirring, or you will release the starch and the rice will become sticky. But you will need to carefully check that the rice is not burning on the bottom of the pan.

5 Meanwhile, heat the remaining oil in a large frying pan over a high heat. Add the marinated lamb and cook, stirring frequently, for about 5 minutes until browned all over. Season with salt and pepper. Toss the lamb with the cooked rice, using a fork so that you don't squash the rice, cover and cook for a further 5 minutes.

6 Fork the coriander and mint through the rice and remove the cinnamon stick and Scotch bonnet chilli just before serving.

I love tomatoes and their sunshine flavours, especially when they have spices on them to wake up your taste buds. This dish hits the spice spot all right - right at the back of the throat! The tomatoes are also great on their own with a bit of toasted Italian bread.

Serves 4

salt

300g (10½oz) dried penne
(or similar shaped pasta)

250g (9oz) mozzarella cheese,
roughly torn

3 tbsp chopped flat leaf parsley
leaves

3 spring onions, green parts only,
finely chopped

1½ tbsp olive oil, to serve

**For the thyme and chilli
roasted tomatoes**

15 plum tomatoes

2 tbsp olive oil

1 tbsp caster sugar

1½ tsp sea salt

1 tsp ground black pepper

1 tsp dried chilli flakes

2 tsp thyme leaves

1 For the roasted tomatoes, preheat the oven to 160°C (fan)/180°C/gas mark 4. Cut the tomatoes into long slices, about 1.5cm (⅝in) thick (about 3-4 per tomato). Pour the oil on to a baking sheet and arrange the tomato slices on top. Mix the sugar, salt, pepper, chilli flakes and thyme together, and sprinkle over the top of the tomato slices. Roast in the oven for 30 minutes.

2 About 20 minutes before the tomatoes are ready, bring a large saucepan of salted water to the boil. Add the pasta and cook according to the packet instructions until *al dente*.

3 Drain the cooked pasta and then mix with the roasted tomatoes, mozzarella, parsley and spring onion greens. Serve in big bowls, drizzled with the olive oil.

Macaroni cheese, more please! Spices add an extra edge to a familiar dish like this – I love the grainy mustard with the macaroni. The tomatoes and the spring onions make it look fantastic, as well as bringing another dimension to the taste. It's great served with a green salad tossed in a sharp dressing.

Serves 4–5

salt

200g (7oz) dried macaroni

550ml (19fl oz) milk

200ml (⅓ pint) double cream

1 bay leaf

generous fresh grating of nutmeg

30g (1oz) butter

30g (1oz) plain flour

150g (5½oz) Cheddar cheese, grated

50g (2oz) Parmesan, freshly grated

2–3 tbsp grainy mustard, or to taste

200g (7oz) cherry tomatoes, halved

3 spring onions, green parts only, finely chopped.

1 Preheat the oven to 140°C (fan)/160°C/gas mark 3. Bring a large saucepan of salted water to the boil. Add the macaroni and cook according to the packet instructions until *al dente*.

2 Put the milk and cream into a small saucepan with the bay leaf and nutmeg. Bring just to the boil, then reduce the heat to very low so that it is just kept warm.

3 Meanwhile, melt the butter in a medium saucepan, add the flour and cook over a low heat, stirring, for 2 minutes. Gradually add the hot creamy milk mixture, stirring hard to make a smooth sauce. Stir in four-fifths of the grated cheeses and all the mustard. Season with a little salt, if necessary, remembering that the macaroni has been cooked in salty water.

4 Drain the cooked macaroni and return to the pan. Pour over the mustardy cheese sauce and stir in the cherry tomatoes and spring onion greens.

5 Pour the macaroni mixture into a large, shallow ovenproof dish and scatter over the remaining cheese. Bake in the oven for 20 minutes or until patched with brown on top.

QUINOA WITH SWEET POTATOES, PEPPERS & AVOCADO PUREE

Quinoa (pronounced Kin-wa) is a South-American grain that makes a good change from rice. Here I have Caribbean-ized it. If you don't want to eat it with the puréed avocado, try an avocado salsa instead. You can also add cooked pulses – kidney beans, black beans or chickpeas – to this dish.

Serves 6

2 red peppers, cored, deseeded and cut into 4cm (1½in) squares

500g (1lb 2oz) sweet potatoes, peeled and cut into 4cm (1½in) chunks

3 tbsp olive oil

1 tbsp cayenne pepper

salt and black pepper

2 tbsp groundnut or sunflower oil

1 small onion, finely chopped

3 tsp ground cinnamon

3 tsp ground ginger

3cm (1¼in) piece of fresh root ginger, grated

3 garlic cloves, finely chopped

300g (10½oz) quinoa

675ml (scant 1¼ pints) chicken or vegetable stock or water

about 8 spring onions, chopped

extra virgin olive oil, to serve

For the avocado purée

2 avocados, chopped

2 garlic cloves, crushed

4 tbsp extra virgin olive oil

2 tbsp lime juice

1 tbsp sherry vinegar

2 tbsp chopped fresh coriander, plus extra leaves to garnish

1 Preheat the oven to 170°C (fan)/190°C/gas mark 5. Put the pepper squares and sweet potato chunks into a roasting tin and toss with the olive oil, cayenne and salt and pepper. Roast in the oven for about 25 minutes or until tender.

2 Meanwhile, heat the groundnut oil in a heavy-based saucepan with a tight-fitting lid over a medium heat. Add the onion and cook, stirring occasionally, until soft and slightly golden.

3 Add the cinnamon, ground and fresh ginger and garlic to the pan and cook, stirring, for 2 minutes. Add the quinoa and season with salt and pepper. Cover with the stock, stir and bring to the boil. Immediately reduce the heat, cover and cook the quinoa on the lowest heat you can for about 15 minutes until it has absorbed all the stock and is quite dry and nutty. Leave the quinoa in the pan.

4 For the avocado purée, put all the ingredients into a blender or food processor and whizz until smooth.

5 Stir the spring onions through the quinoa and put the roasted vegetables on top. Serve with the avocado purée, drizzled with a little extra virgin olive oil and garnished with coriander leaves.

06

Plain old carrot soup is given a bit of a kick in this recipe with the addition of some chopped red chillies, and it's topped off in style with a lime and coriander-flavoured cream. If you have one of those mini food processors, you can whizz the cream ingredients up in that to produce a lovely green sauce.

Serves 4

25g (1oz) butter

2 tsp sunflower oil

1 onion, finely chopped

1 celery stick, finely chopped

3 garlic cloves, finely sliced

2 red chillies, deseeded and chopped

2.5cm (1in) piece of fresh root ginger, peeled and finely chopped

10 carrots, peeled and cut into big chunks

1 litre (1¾ pints) chicken or vegetable stock, plus extra if needed

salt and black pepper

For the coriander cream

125ml (4fl oz) double cream

juice of 1 lime

1 tbsp chopped fresh coriander

1 Heat the butter with the oil in a saucepan over a medium-low heat, add the onion and celery and cook, stirring occasionally, until soft and pale gold. Add the garlic, chillies and ginger and cook, stirring, for 2-3 minutes.

2 Add the carrots and stock and bring to the boil. Reduce the heat and simmer for about 30 minutes or until the carrots are completely tender. Leave to cool slightly, then purée with a stick blender or in a blender or food processor. If the consistency is too thick, add a little more stock. Reheat the soup and check the seasoning.

3 For the coriander cream, mix the cream, lime juice and coriander together and season to taste. Serve the soup with some of the coriander cream added to each portion.

I've cooked cakes with Angostura bitters and love the flavour it can give to dishes. Then the food writer Xanthe Clay recommended it in a sweet potato soup, so I tried it out – delicious! The bitters merge beautifully with the sweet root, as does the ginger here.

Serves 4

2 tbsp olive oil

1 small onion, finely chopped

1 garlic clove, finely chopped

2 celery sticks, sliced

salt and black pepper

600g (1lb 5oz) sweet potatoes (2 large or 3 medium)

6cm (2½in) piece of fresh root ginger, peeled and finely chopped

750ml (1⅓ pints) chicken or vegetable stock

2 bay leaves

2 tsp Angostura bitters

juice of 1 lime

double cream, to serve (optional)

1 Heat the oil in a large saucepan over a medium-low heat, add the onion, garlic and celery with a pinch of salt and cook, stirring occasionally, until soft.

2 Meanwhile, peel the sweet potatoes and cut into 4cm (1½in) chunks.

3 Add the sweet potatoes to the pan with the ginger and cook, stirring occasionally, for 2 minutes. Add the stock and bay leaves and bring to the boil, then reduce the heat and simmer, covered, for 40 minutes.

4 Leave the soup to cool slightly, then purée with a stick blender or in a blender or food processor. Add the Angostura bitters and lime juice, tasting as you go and adding more salt and pepper if necessary as well. Reheat the soup, then serve with a swirl of cream, if you like, or leave it just as it is, golden orange in the bowl.

GINGER & CORIANDER GLAZED CARROTS

These are the best carrots I've tried - carrots fabulocious! I like their sweetness so much. I'd happily eat them on their own as a starter. But really this is an accompaniment to fish or meat. Coriander - both leaf and seed - goes really well with carrots, as does ginger, so this is double-nice with the spice.

Serves 4 as a side dish

1 tsp coriander seeds

25g (1oz) butter

2 tbsp stem ginger syrup

2 tbsp water

4 carrots, peeled and cut into batons

salt and black pepper

1 Heat a heavy-based saucepan over a low heat, add the coriander seeds and toast, shaking the pan occasionally, until fragrant.

2 Melt the butter in a medium saucepan. Add the ginger syrup and the water, then stir in the carrot batons and season with salt and pepper.

3 Cover and cook over a very low heat for 10 minutes, stirring once or twice. Take the lid off and continue cooking for a few more minutes until the liquid has mostly evaporated and the carrots are nicely glazed.

This is a lovely Caribbean-flavoured curry using all the root veg we get here in Britain during the autumn and winter. Parsnips have never tasted so good! You can use waxy or floury potatoes - you'll just get different results.

Serves 8

2 tbsp sunflower or groundnut oil

3 onions, finely chopped

4 garlic cloves, crushed

4cm (1½in) piece of fresh root ginger, peeled and finely chopped

1 Scotch bonnet chilli, deseeded and chopped

1½ tsp ground coriander

1 tsp ground turmeric

1 cinnamon stick, broken in half

salt and black pepper

300g (10½oz) each of carrots, parsnips and sweet potatoes, peeled and cut into 3cm (1¼in) chunks

400g (14oz) potatoes, peeled and cut into 3cm (1¼in) chunks

1 litre (1¾ pints) vegetable stock

2 tbsp tomato purée

2 bay leaves

pinch of soft dark brown sugar

75g (2¾oz) cashew nuts, crushed, plus extra, chopped, to serve

100g (3½oz) French beans, topped and tailed, then halved

200g (7oz) baby spinach leaves

4 tbsp double cream

juice of 1 lime

To serve

Mango & Coconut Relish (*see* page 166)

warm rotis (optional)

1 Heat the oil in a flameproof casserole dish over a medium heat. Add the onions and cook, stirring occasionally, until they are a good brown colour – make sure they do not burn. Add the garlic, ginger and chilli and cook, stirring frequently, for about 5 minutes, then add the spices with ½ teaspoon pepper and cook, stirring, for another minute to release their fragrance.

2 Stir in all the root vegetables. Cook, stirring occasionally, for about 4 minutes, then add the stock, tomato purée, bay leaves and sugar, followed by the crushed nuts. Season with salt and pepper and bring to just under the boil. Reduce the heat to a steady simmer and cook for about 15 minutes until the vegetables are almost tender. You may have to add a little water if the mixture starts to get dry, but the sauce should just coat the vegetables.

3 Add the beans and spinach for about the last 3 minutes of the cooking time, then stir in the cream. Taste and add half the lime juice, then adjust the seasoning and decide whether you want to add any more lime juice.

4 Serve the root curry piping hot, scattered with chopped cashews, with the Mango & Coconut Relish on the side, together with warm rotis for dipping, if you like.

SUNSHINE BAKED SWEET POTATOES WITH SPICY SAUSAGE

Perfect for those evenings when you just want a baked potato, this is like having your breakfast and supper all in one. You can use bacon instead of sausage if you prefer, and leave out the cheese if you're not keen on it – but don't leave out the chilli!

Serves 2

2 large sweet potatoes, about 300–350g (10½–12oz) each

40g (1½oz) butter

2 spicy pork sausages, chopped into 2cm (¾in) chunks

½ small onion, finely chopped

1 red chilli, deseeded and finely chopped

30g (1oz) Cheddar cheese, grated

1½ tbsp roughly chopped fresh coriander (optional)

salt and black pepper

2 small eggs

cayenne pepper, to garnish

1 Preheat the oven to 180°C (fan)/200°C/gas mark 6. Wash the sweet potatoes, then set them directly on the oven shelf or in a small roasting tin and bake for about 50 minutes until tender right through the centre – test by inserting a sharp pointed knife.

2 While the potatoes are cooking, heat 25g (1oz) of the butter in a frying pan until foaming. Add the sausage and onion and cook over a medium heat, stirring occasionally, for about 8 minutes until the onion is soft and golden and the sausage is cooked through. Add the chilli and cook, stirring, for another minute.

3 When the potatoes are tender, halve them lengthways without cutting all the way through the skin, so that the potato halves are 'hinged' together. Carefully scoop out the flesh, leaving a thick layer intact so that the skins do not collapse, and mash the flesh in a bowl. Mix the fried onion and sausage, Cheddar, coriander (if using) and salt and pepper into the sweet potato mash.

4 Pile the mash back into the potato halves. Make a little hollow on top of each potato half. Carefully break an egg into each hollow. Season with salt and pepper and add a knob of the remaining butter to each potato.

5 Place the potatoes on a baking tray and return to the oven. Bake for 15 minutes or until the eggs have set. Sprinkle each baked egg with a little salt and cayenne pepper to garnish and serve immediately.

FRIED SWEET POTATOES WITH CAYENNE, CORIANDER & TOASTED COCONUT

The spices, herbs and fresh coconut used here transform the ordinary sweet potato into something magnificent. Some supermarkets are now selling little packets of fresh coconut, so you don't have to crack open a whole one to enjoy this dish.

Serves 4

800g (1lb 12oz) sweet potatoes, cut into 5cm (2in) chunks

25g (1oz) fresh coconut flesh

1 tsp cumin seeds

12 allspice berries

2 tsp cayenne pepper

¼ tsp dried chilli flakes

salt

2 tbsp groundnut or sunflower oil

1 tbsp chopped fresh coriander

1 Put the sweet potatoes into a saucepan of water and bring to the boil, then reduce the heat and simmer for 15 minutes until tender. Drain and return to the saucepan. Cover the potatoes with a clean tea towel, taking care to tuck the entire tea towel into the saucepan, then put the saucepan lid back on. Set the saucepan over a low heat for 3 minutes until the potatoes have dried out a little. Leave to cool, then cut into smaller chunks – about 2.5cm (1in).

2 Using a very fine sharp knife, cut the pieces of coconut flesh into shavings. They do not have to be paper thin, as it is nice if they still have a little crunch once cooked.

3 Use a pestle and mortar to grind all the spices together and sprinkle the spice mix all over the potatoes. Season with salt.

4 Heat 1½ tablespoons of the oil in a frying pan over a medium heat, add the potato chunks and cook, stirring occasionally, for about 6 minutes until golden all over.

5 Meanwhile, heat the remaining oil in a small frying pan over a medium heat, add the coconut shavings and cook until they look just toasted.

6 Toss the coriander with the potatoes and scatter the coconut on top. Serve immediately.

In Jamaica, the standard Brit spud is called an Irish potato, as opposed to the more usual sweet potato. This is a great chilli-hot version of the Sunday lunch classic that you can either eat with a roast or serve with another dish. You could even put them on the table with a few beers and some soured cream for dipping - lovely!

Serves 6

6 floury potatoes (such as King Edwards), peeled

4 tbsp olive oil

1 tbsp plain flour

salt

2–3 red chillies (ideally Scotch Bonnet), finely chopped, with seeds

1 Preheat the oven to 180°C (fan)/200°C/gas mark 6. Cut the potatoes into 4 or 5 equal-sized pieces. Put into a saucepan of water and bring to the boil, then reduce the heat and simmer for 10 minutes. Meanwhile, heat the oil in a shallow roasting tin in the oven.

2 In a colander, drain the potatoes and toss with the flour. Add to the hot fat and turn to coat. Season with salt and toss with the chopped chilli. Roast in the oven for 40-60 minutes, turning over in the fat after about 20 minutes. Season again, if necessary, but they sure won't need more chilli if you have used enough bonnet!

Lordahmercy! This is a good one - warm and spicy, and perfect for a wintry day. You can use other similar vegetables, such as swede and parsnip - just stick to the same quantities. If you have my book, Caribbean Food Made Easy, try this with my Haggis MctumpIings.

Serves 4

125g (4½oz) carrots

450g (1lb) sweet potatoes

200g (7oz) potatoes for mashing (such as King Edwards)

125g (4½oz) parsnips

salt

50g (1¾oz) butter

1 red chilli, deseeded and finely chopped

¼ tsp cayenne pepper

¼ tsp ground cinnamon

¼ tsp ground allspice

good fresh grating of nutmeg

2 tbsp milk

black pepper

½ tbsp chopped fresh coriander

1 Peel all the root vegetables and then cut the carrots into fine slices and all the other vegetables into 3cm (1¼in) chunks.

2 Cook the sweet potatoes and parsnips together (as they take about the same length of time) in a large saucepan of salted boiling water for about 10 minutes or until tender. Meanwhile, cook the potatoes and carrots together in a separate saucepan of salted boiling water for about 15 minutes or until tender. Drain all the vegetables and return them to the large saucepan.

3 Melt the butter in a small saucepan, add all the spices and cook over a medium heat, stirring, for 2 minutes.

4 Mash the vegetables, and as you do so, mix in the milk. Add the spiced butter and plenty of salt and pepper and mash everything together well. Transfer to a warmed serving dish and scatter with the coriander.

SWEET RUM, BUTTER & THYME BAKED ONIONS

I love the soft, sweet flesh of onions, but this treatment, where they're slow-baked in a bit of booze with sprigs of fresh thyme, takes them to a whole new level.

Serves 4

4 onions, halved horizontally, with some of their skin left on

150ml (¼ pint) dark rum

150ml (¼ pint) sweet sherry

125ml (4fl oz) water

35g (1¼oz) unsalted butter

salt and black pepper

juice of 1 lime

about 6 sprigs of thyme

4 tsp soft dark brown sugar

1 Preheat the oven to 160°C (fan)/180°C/gas mark 4. Put the onions into a heatproof gratin dish or a small roasting tin in which they fit snugly in a single layer. Mix the alcohol with the water in a measuring jug.

2 Melt the butter in a small saucepan and then drizzle it over the top of the onions. Season with salt and pepper, then add the lime juice and half the alcohol and water mixture. Scatter the thyme sprigs over the top.

3 Bake in the oven for 50 minutes, basting occasionally with the juices. Baste with the remaining alcohol and water mixture when the onions become dry.

4 When the onions have another 20 minutes still to cook, sprinkle over the sugar and then continue baking. The alcohol and water mixture should reduce and be absorbed by the onions as they cook. They are ready when they are tender – pierce with a sharp knife to check – and golden brown.

07

These satisfying stuffed peppers make a great side dish, but can also be served as a vegetarian main course, in which case you will need to serve **2** or **3** halves to each person, according to the size of their appetite, and accompany with a crisp, green salad.

Serves 8 as a side dish

8 red peppers

olive oil

2 aubergines

salt and black pepper

1 red chilli, deseeded and finely sliced

2 garlic cloves, crushed

3 tsp cayenne pepper

½ tsp ground cumin

400g can black beans, drained and rinsed

juice of ½ lemon

2 tbsp finely chopped fresh coriander

To serve

extra virgin olive oil (optional)

sweet paprika

1 Preheat the oven to 180°C (fan)/200°C/gas mark 6. Cut the peppers in half lengthways. Remove the stalks and pull out the cores and seeds. Put the peppers into a shallow roasting tin in which they fit in a single layer (use 2 if necessary) and drizzle with about 5 tablespoons olive oil. Turn the peppers to coat well in the oil. Roast for 35-40 minutes or until completely soft and a little charred round the edges.

2 While the peppers are cooking, cut the aubergines into 1.5cm (⅝in) chunks. Heat 3 tablespoons olive oil in a frying pan over a high heat, add the aubergines and cook for about 5 minutes, stirring from time to time, until golden. Reduce the heat to medium and cook for another 5-7 minutes until soft. You will need to add more olive oil as the aubergines cook, because their flesh drinks such a lot of it, but try not to add too much or the dish will be oily (the aubergines eventually throw out a lot of the liquid that they have taken in during cooking).

3 Season the aubergines well with salt and pepper, add the chilli, garlic, cayenne and cumin and cook, stirring, for another 2 minutes. Add the black beans and lemon juice and heat through. Add the coriander and check the seasoning.

4 Fill the roasted peppers with the stuffing. Serve the stuffed peppers either warm or at room temperature, drizzled with a little extra virgin olive oil, if you like, and sprinkled with paprika.

This gutsy tomato chutney is terrific in cheese sandwiches. To skin the tomatoes, make a cross at the base of each, put them into a bowl of just-boiled water and leave for 5 minutes. Drain and just peel away the softened skins when they are cool enough to handle.

Makes 350g (12oz) or 3 × 250ml (9fl oz) jars

900g (2lb) tomatoes, skinned and roughly chopped

225g (8oz) onion, roughly chopped

6 garlic cloves, chopped

2 red chillies, deseeded and finely chopped

3cm (1¼in) cube of fresh root ginger, peeled and finely chopped

2 red peppers, cored, deseeded and chopped into 1.5cm (⅝in) pieces

400ml (14fl oz) distilled white vinegar

250g (9oz) demerara sugar

salt

1 Put all the ingredients into a saucepan and slowly bring to the boil over a medium heat, stirring a little to help the sugar dissolve.

2 Cook gently, uncovered, for about 1½ hours until the mixture is tender and chutney-like.

3 Towards the end of the cooking time, sterilize your jars and lids ready for potting – you need to use glass or plastic (acid or vinegar-proof) lids. Preheat the oven to 130°C (fan)/150°C/gas mark 2. Wash the jars and lids in plenty of warm, soapy water. Rinse, dry and stand in a large roasting tin. Heat them in the oven for 15 minutes. Alternatively, run them through a regular dishwasher cycle.

4 Pot the chutney into the still-warm but dry sterilized jars. Cover and seal with the lids. Store in a cool, dark place and consume within a year. Once opened, refrigerate and use within 6 months.

Cool as a cucumber and hot as a chilli, this is a great condiment to have alongside a nice piece of fish. The relish can be made a day in advance, but it's best eaten on the same day.

Serves 6

1 large cucumber

salt

3 tbsp caster sugar

2 tbsp white wine vinegar

2 tbsp finely chopped dill

½–¾ tsp deseeded and finely chopped red chilli (ideally Scotch bonnet)

1 Peel the cucumber, cut in half lengthways and then scoop the seeds out of each half with a teaspoon. Sprinkle generously with salt and leave for 30 minutes. Briefly rinse and pat dry with kitchen paper.

2 Meanwhile, mix the sugar and vinegar together and leave to stand, stirring occasionally, until the sugar has dissolved. Stir in the dill and the chilli, to taste.

3 Finely slice the cucumber and put into a shallow ceramic dish. Pour over the dressing. Cover and leave in the fridge until ready to eat.

This is good either hot or cold. It tastes slightly Indian even though it's creole. You can make it daringly hot by adding a couple of fresh chillies - cook them with the aubergine once it has softened.

Serves 8

6 tbsp olive oil

2 onions, roughly chopped

4 garlic cloves, finely chopped

1 green pepper, cored, deseeded and cut into 2cm (¾in) squares

1 red pepper, cored, deseeded and cut into 2cm (¾in) squares

3 large aubergines, cut into 3cm (1¼in) cubes

1 tsp hot paprika

1 tsp sweet paprika

2 tsp ground cumin

2 × 395g cans cherry tomatoes in thick juice

½ tsp soft light brown sugar, or to taste

salt and black pepper

350ml (12fl oz) water

2 tbsp chopped flat leaf parsley

lime wedges, to serve (optional)

1 Heat 2 tablespoons of the oil in a frying pan over a medium heat, add the onions, garlic and peppers and cook, stirring occasionally, until soft, about 12 minutes.

2 Meanwhile, heat the remaining oil in a sauté pan or flameproof casserole dish over a medium-high heat, add the aubergines and cook, stirring occasionally, for about 10 minutes until golden all over.

3 Add the paprikas and cumin to the onion mixture and cook, stirring, for 1 minute, then add the tomatoes, sugar, aubergines and salt and pepper. Top up with the water and bring to the boil. Reduce the heat and simmer for 15-20 minutes until the mixture is thick and cooked through. Sprinkle with the chopped parsley and serve with lime wedges, if you like.

Here's a gorgeous dish that's good enough to bring cauliflower back into favour, even if you think you don't like it - it's the opposite of soggy school-dinner bland. Nutmeg and cauliflower is a combination made in heaven. Serve with a yogurty or hot chilli dip, or as a side dish with a piece of salmon or fried chicken.

Serves 3–4 as a snack

1 large cauliflower

4 tbsp sunflower or olive oil

½ tsp freshly grated nutmeg

¼–½ tsp chilli powder

¼ tsp ground black pepper

½ tsp salt

1 Preheat the oven to 170°C (fan)/190°C/gas mark 5. Break the cauliflower into small florets and cut any remaining stem into medium chunks.

2 Mix the oil with the spices and salt in a large bowl. Add the cauliflower and toss well to combine.

3 Put the spiced-up cauliflower on a baking sheet and roast in the oven for 25–30 minutes until crispy brown on the edges, turning over a couple of times during the cooking time. Serve immediately.

Chilled tomato soup to most people, this is love apple soup to me. It's great to make for friends in the summer, as you can cook it well in advance, although make the salsa at the last minute otherwise it will lose its crunchiness.

Serves 8

4 tbsp olive oil

1 large onion, finely chopped

1 celery stick, finely chopped

2 garlic cloves, finely chopped

1 red chilli, deseeded and finely chopped

2kg (4lb 8oz) plum tomatoes, roughly chopped

850ml (1½ pints) water, plus extra if necessary

1½ tbsp soft light brown sugar

salt and black pepper

3 tbsp extra virgin olive oil, or to taste

For the salsa

½ large cucumber

juice of 1 lime

½–1 tsp caster sugar

2 tbsp chopped mint leaves

1½ tbsp extra virgin olive oil

salt and black pepper

1 Heat 2 tablespoons of the olive oil in a heavy-based saucepan over a medium-low heat. Add the onion and celery and cook, stirring occasionally, until soft but not coloured – about 7–10 minutes. Add the garlic and chilli and cook, stirring, for 2 minutes.

2 Add the chopped tomatoes, water, sugar and salt and pepper to taste to the pan, then bring to the boil. Immediately reduce the heat and leave the soup to simmer for about 30 minutes. You need to keep an eye on the pan so that it does not boil dry or you will burn the tomatoes, and add a little water when you have to. Leave the soup to cool.

3 Check the soup for seasoning and add the extra virgin olive oil. Transfer the soup to a food processor (not a blender, as that would break up the seeds of the tomatoes) and whizz until puréed, then push the mixture through a sieve to remove the seeds. You may find you need a little more water or want some more extra virgin olive oil in the soup. Cover and leave to chill in the fridge.

4 For the salsa, cut the cucumber in half lengthways and then scoop the seeds out of each half with a teaspoon. Dice the flesh and mix with all the remaining ingredients. Taste for seasoning and adjust if necessary.

5 Serve the soup cold with a big spoonful of the salsa on top of each serving.

This dish uses the big, meaty tomatoes that some people call beefsteak but I know as Jamaican salad tomatoes. I've spiced them up with thyme leaves, salt and black pepper to make a crunchy topping that works a treat. Serve this as a starter with some salad or bread, or alongside some meat or fish as a main course.

Serves 4 as a starter or side dish

2 beefsteak tomatoes

4 tbsp olive oil, plus extra for oiling the roasting tin

75g (2¾oz) white bread

1 scant tsp finely grated orange rind

3 tsp roughly chopped thyme leaves

sea salt and black pepper

1 Preheat the oven to 180°C (fan)/200°C/gas mark 6. Cut each tomato into 4 thick slices. Lightly brush a shallow roasting tin with olive oil and add the tomatoes. Roast for 15 minutes.

2 Meanwhile, whizz the bread into breadcrumbs in a food processor. Put into a bowl and mix thoroughly with the orange rind, thyme and a seasoning of salt and plenty of pepper. Pour in the oil and mix it in well (it helps to do this with your hands rather than a spoon).

3 Remove the tomatoes from the oven and pat about 1 tablespoon of the breadcrumb mixture down on to each slice. Return to the oven and cook for another 15 minutes or until crispy brown on top. Sprinkle with extra sea salt to serve.

Globe artichokes are very 'ital', meaning 'vital' food - healthy and fresh. These look like small beasts on the barbecue and taste really good. You can also roast them in the oven.

Serves 4

4 globe artichokes

4 tbsp olive oil

1 tsp salt

½ tsp ground black pepper

1½ tsp smoked paprika

1 juicy lime, cut into quarters, for squeezing over

1 To trim the artichokes, cut off each stem down to the base of the leaves. Turn each artichoke upside down and press down on a work surface several times to open up the leaves, then spread them out with your fingers to open them up a bit more.

2 Mix the oil with the salt, pepper and smoked paprika. Drizzle the spiced oil into the open leaves, trying to get it into as much of the artichoke as possible. (If your artichokes are big ones, increase the amount of dressing.)

3 Nestle the artichoke in the barbecue ashes and leave for about an hour until tender. Alternatively, bake in an oven preheated to 180°C (fan)/200°C/gas mark 6 for an hour or until tender.

4 Serve with a napkin for holding the artichoke while you pull off the leaves and eat the little tender base at the end of each leaf. When you get to the hairy centre, or choke, cut it off with a knife, pull it away with your fingers and then eat the heart.

Haloumi is great for a barbecue, whether you're veggie or not. It goes all brown and crispy without melting, and here I've put it in pitta breads with chargrilled red onions and lots of sauce incorporating the flavours of the haloumi marinade. The dressing is quite sharp, but it works well with the sweetness of the onions.

Serves 4 as part of a barbecue

250g (9oz) haloumi cheese

2 red onions

4 pitta breads

rocket leaves, to serve

For the lime and bay marinade

juice of 2 limes

4 bay leaves, roughly torn

¼ tsp ground allspice

1 tsp ground black pepper

2 tbsp olive oil

For the dressing

4 tbsp Greek yogurt

¼ garlic clove, crushed (optional)

1 Mix all the marinade ingredients together in a shallow ceramic dish. Slice the haloumi cheese into 8 × 2.5-3cm (1-1¼in) thick cubes (slice the cheese into quarters and then each quarter in half). Cut the ends off the onions, peel off the skin and cut them crossways into 3cm (1¼in) thick pieces so that each onion is a nest of circles. Add the haloumi and onions to the marinade and turn until well coated. Cover and leave to marinate at room temperature for 2 hours, spooning the marinade over a couple of times.

2 Light a barbecue. Soak 8 bamboo skewers in cold water for at least 30 minutes. Lift the haloumi and onions out of the marinade.

3 For the dressing, mix the marinade with the yogurt and the garlic (if using) and set aside.

4 Thread 2 pieces of haloumi on to 4 skewers and 2 pieces of onion on to the remaining 4 skewers. When the flames from the barbecue have died down and the coals are glowing, put the skewers on the grill. Cook until browned, turning over a few times. The onions will take longer than the haloumi, about 6-7 minutes on each side; the haloumi more like 3-5 minutes on each side, depending on the heat of your barbecue. (If you like, you can instead thread a single piece of haloumi and onion on to each skewer and move them around the barbecue so that the onions are on the hotter part of the barbecue.)

5 Warm the pitta breads on the grill, turning over once. Take the haloumi and onions off the skewers and serve in the pitta breads with rocket leaves and spoonfuls of the dressing.

Wow! This is definitely one up on carrot cake if you ask me. It's perfect for having with a mug of coffee in front of a roaring fire on a cold day.

Serves 8

500g (1lb 2oz) deseeded crown prince pumpkin or butternut squash, skin on

50ml (2fl oz) milk

125g (4½oz) unsalted butter, softened, plus extra for greasing

300g (10½oz) plain flour

2 tsp baking powder

½ tsp bicarbonate of soda

good pinch of salt

1 tsp ground cinnamon

½ tsp freshly grated nutmeg

½ tsp ground ginger

¼ tsp ground cloves

¼ tsp ground allspice

275g (9½oz) soft dark brown sugar

2 large eggs, lightly beaten

75g (2¾oz) dried cranberries

75g (2¾oz) toasted pecan nuts, chopped, plus extra to serve

For the buttercream

200g (7oz) unsalted butter, slightly softened

400g (14oz) soft light brown sugar

finely grated rind and juice of ½ orange

1 Preheat the oven to 170°C (fan)/190°C/gas mark 5. Cut the pumpkin or squash into wedges, arrange in a roasting tin in a single layer and bake in the oven for 45–60 minutes – it needs to be really golden and dried out or else the cake will not cook properly. Remove the skin from the pumpkin, put the flesh into a blender with the milk and whizz until completely smooth.

2 Reduce the oven temperature to 160°C (fan)/180°C/gas mark 4. Line the bases of 2 × 20cm (8in) round cake tins with greaseproof paper, then grease the tins with butter.

3 Sift the flour, baking powder, bicarbonate of soda, salt and ground spices together.

4 Beat the butter and sugar together in a large mixing bowl until light and fluffy. Beat in the eggs a little at a time. If the mixture starts to curdle, mix in a tablespoon of the flour mixture. Fold in the flour mixture alternately with the pumpkin purée using a large metal spoon. Stir in the cranberries and pecans.

5 Divide the cake mixture between the prepared tins, spreading it level. Bake for 25 minutes or until a skewer inserted into the centre of the cakes comes out clean.

6 Leave the cakes to cool in the tins for 10 minutes, then turn them out on to a wire rack, peel off the lining paper and leave to cool completely.

7 For the buttercream, beat the butter with an electric whisk until light and fluffy, then beat in the sugar. Finally, beat in the orange rind and juice. Put one cake on a serving plate. Spread half the buttercream over it using a palette knife, then put the other cake on top. Spread the remaining buttercream over the top, then scatter with extra pecans to decorate. The cake is ready to serve.

I call these my Bling Buns because they sparkle with diamonds of sugar on top. They taste a little like old-fashioned cinnamon toast - this is food at its comfiest.

Makes 16 buns

450ml (16fl oz) warm water (100ml/4fl oz just boiled and 350ml/12fl oz cold)

1 tbsp dried yeast (not easy-blend)

1 tsp caster sugar

750g (1lb 10oz) strong white flour, plus extra for dusting

15g (½oz) butter

1 tsp salt

sunflower oil, for oiling

For the cinnamon butter filling

150g (5½oz) butter, softened

150g (5½oz) crunchy Barbados or demerara sugar

1½–2 tsp ground cinnamon

For the bling glaze

½ large egg, beaten

1½–2 tbsp crunchy Barbados or demerara sugar

1 Measure the water into a jug and whisk in the yeast and sugar. Leave for 10 minutes until it is frothy (this proves that the yeast is active). Put three-quarters of the flour, all the butter and the salt into the bowl of an electric mixer with a dough hook and knead on a low speed for 15 seconds until combined. Add the yeasty water mixture and mix for 2 minutes, then add the remaining flour and mix until the dough is smooth and elastic. If preparing by hand, put the flour, butter and salt into a large mixing bowl. Make a well in the centre and add the warm yeasty water to the centre. Stir the ingredients into the water using a knife and then using your hand. Knead for 10–15 minutes on a lightly floured surface until the dough is elastic and smooth.

2 Put the dough into a clean, lightly oiled bowl, cover with a clean tea towel and leave to rise in a warm place for 2 hours until about doubled in size.

3 Meanwhile, make the cinnamon butter filling by roughly mixing all the ingredients together.

4 Knock back the dough by punching it to remove the air so that it returns to its original size, then turn out on to a floured work surface. Roll out into a long oblong about 30cm × 40cm × 1cm (12in × 16in × ½in). Dot the filling all over the oblong. Roll up along the long side into a sausage. Cut into 16 equal pieces. Put these on to a baking sheet in 3 long rows (6 in the centre and 5 on either side), with a gap of a few centimetres between the rows and a small gap between the buns. Leave to rise in a warm place for another 30 minutes. Preheat the oven to 200°C (fan)/220°C/gas mark 7.

5 For the glaze, brush the buns with the beaten egg, then sprinkle over the sugar. Bake for about 20 minutes or until golden. Leave to cool slightly in the tin, then remove, break apart and leave to cool on a wire rack.

CARDAMOM, HONEY & VANILLA FUDGE

A truly sunsational combination! The aromatic cardamom somehow stops the fudge being too sweet and the honey adds a warm buzz. It makes a great present for friends and family, or have it at home with coffee after supper.

Makes 16–24 squares – portion depends on your sweet tooth!

400g (14oz) granulated sugar

400g can condensed milk

100ml (3½fl oz) water

pinch of salt

3 tbsp clear honey

seeds from 5 cardamom pods, crushed

sunflower oil, for oiling

2 tsp vanilla extract

60g (2¼oz) unsalted butter, diced

1 Put the sugar, condensed milk and water into a large, heavy-based saucepan. Heat gently, stirring a little, until the sugar has dissolved. Stir in the salt, honey and cardamom.

2 Increase the heat, bring to the boil and continue boiling, stirring frequently to ensure that it does not burn on the bottom. After a few minutes, put a sugar thermometer into the pan, and when it reaches 116°C/241°F, turn the heat off and leave to cool slightly. Meanwhile, lightly oil a 20cm (8in) square shallow baking tin.

3 Stir in the vanilla extract and butter. Beat vigorously and as the fudge cools it will thicken and become grainy. Pour into the tin and leave to cool, then mark off and cut into squares. Serve in mini petit four cases, if you like.

Here's a Sunday afternoon sort of a cake, one to eat watching the cricket, or else have it warm for pudding with lashings of cream or ice cream. Pear and ginger is a classic combination, and the honey gives a nice warmth to the flavour. Three kinds of ginger are used - root, stem and ground - to give the cake a triple dose of this delicious ingredient.

Serves 8

200g (7oz) unsalted butter, plus extra for greasing

100g (3½oz) light muscovado sugar

150g (5½oz) light clear honey

1 tsp ground ginger

4cm (1½in) piece of fresh root ginger, peeled and grated

3 bulbs of stem ginger in syrup, finely chopped

3 large eggs, lightly beaten

200g (7oz) self-raising flour

3 pears, peeled, cored and chopped into small chunks (these don't have to be perfectly ripe, but it's better if they're not hard)

1 Preheat the oven to 170°C (fan)/190°C/gas mark 5. Grease the sides and base of a 23cm (9in) round cake tin with a removable base and line the sides with baking paper.

2 Melt the butter in a saucepan, then stir in the sugar and honey. Transfer to a mixing bowl. Add the ground ginger, grated root ginger and stem ginger and stir thoroughly. Add the eggs and stir in well. Sift in the flour and fold in with a large metal spoon, then fold in the pears.

3 Pour the cake mixture into the prepared tin and set it on a baking sheet. Bake in the oven for 1¼ hours or until a skewer inserted into the centre of the cake comes out clean. This is great served warm or cold.

BANANA, CHOCOLATE & RUM ICE CREAM

This ice cream is an amazing flavour experience - you really can taste every luscious ingredient in it. It's also not overly sweet, so it's especially good for serving to grown-ups.

Serves 6

115g (4oz) plain dark chocolate, broken into small pieces

185ml (6½fl oz) milk

150ml (¼ pint) double cream

3 tbsp soft dark brown sugar

¼ tsp ground cinnamon

finely grated rind of 1 orange

juice of ½ an orange

4 small very ripe bananas, peeled and sliced

50ml (2fl oz) curaçao

3 tbsp dark rum

1 Put the chocolate, milk, cream, sugar and cinnamon in a saucepan and heat gently until melted. Stir in the orange rind and juice, then leave to cool. Transfer to a blender with the bananas, curaçao and rum and whizz until smooth.

2 Pour the mixture into an ice cream machine and churn according to the manufacturer's instructions. If you don't have an ice cream machine, pour the mixture into a shallow container - preferably metal, as it conducts the coldness well - and put it into the coldest part of your freezer for 6-7 hours until firm. Beat the ice cream with a fork or an electric whisk about 5 times during the freezing process to ensure a smooth, creamy ice cream. Serve in scoops in glasses or small dishes.

SPICED CHOCOLATE LURVE CAKE

This fabulous cake isn't just for someone you love - it's for someone you want to love you! Bake this for them and they'll be unable to resist you. If you feel like going over the top - and sometimes I do - spread a layer of raspberry jam in the middle as well as filling it with cream and fruit.

Serves 8

225g (8oz) butter, softened, plus extra for greasing

225g (8oz) soft dark brown sugar

4 large eggs, lightly beaten

1 tsp vanilla extract

165g (5¾oz) self-raising flour, sifted

75g (2¾oz) cocoa powder, sifted

5 tsp ground cinnamon

2 tsp ground allspice

For the chocolate icing

75g (2¾oz) milk chocolate, broken into small pieces

75g (2¾oz) plain dark chocolate, broken into small pieces

1 tbsp soft dark brown sugar

150ml (¼ pint) soured cream

1 tsp ground cinnamon

2 tbsp white rum

For the filling

250ml (9fl oz) double cream

½ tbsp white rum, or to taste

4 tbsp icing sugar

250g (9oz) fresh raspberries

To decorate

250g (9oz) fresh raspberries

icing sugar, for dusting

1 Preheat the oven to 160°C (fan)/180°C/gas mark 4. Grease a 23–25cm (9–10in) heart-shaped cake tin with butter and line the base with greaseproof paper.

2 Beat the butter and sugar together in a large mixing bowl until light and fluffy. Gradually beat in the eggs a little at a time. Beat in the vanilla extract, then fold in the flour, cocoa powder and spices with a large metal spoon. Pour the cake mixture into the prepared tin and bake for about 30 minutes or until a skewer inserted into the centre of the cake comes out clean. Turn the cake out on to a wire rack and leave to cool completely.

3 For the icing, put the chocolate in a heatproof bowl set over a saucepan of barely simmering water, making sure that the bottom of the bowl does not touch the water. When the chocolate has melted, add the sugar, soured cream, cinnamon and rum. Beat with a wooden spoon until the mixture becomes perfectly smooth. Leave to cool and firm up.

4 For the filling, whip the cream until it forms medium peaks, then fold in the rum and icing sugar with a large metal spoon.

5 When the cake is cool, cut it in half horizontally with a large sharp knife. Peel off the lining paper from the bottom half of the cake and set, cut-side up, on a cake stand or plate. Spread the filling on to the cake to within about 2.5cm (1in) of the edge. Top with the raspberries for the filling, sift over icing sugar to taste, then cover with the top cake layer, cut-side down.

6 Spoon the icing on to the top of the cake and then spread it over to cover. Arrange the raspberries for decorating all over the top of the cake. Sift a light dusting of icing sugar over the top and serve.

WHITE CHOCOLATE & VANILLA MOUSSE WITH A STRAWBERRY & BLACK PEPPERCORN SAUCE

This mousse is perfect for summer. Believe me, the pepper really brings out another taste in the strawberries - that's spice magic! It's simple to make and very popular with everyone who eats it. If you don't want to prepare the sauce, serve it with fresh fruit.

Serves 4–6

200g (7oz) white chocolate, broken into small pieces

1 tsp vanilla extract

150ml (¼ pint) whipping cream

3 large egg whites

For the strawberry and black peppercorn sauce

100g (3½oz) caster sugar

200ml (⅓ pint) water

1–2 tsp ground black pepper

400g (14oz) fresh strawberries, hulled and roughly chopped

1 Melt the chocolate in a microwave on a low setting or by putting into a heatproof bowl set over a saucepan of barely simmering water, making sure that the bottom of the bowl does not touch the water. Stir in the vanilla extract and leave to cool slightly.

2 Meanwhile, whip the cream until it forms soft peaks. Wash your whisk carefully and dry it thoroughly, then use it to whisk the egg whites in a separate large bowl until stiff. Fold the cream into the melted chocolate, then add a tablespoonful of the egg whites to the chocolate mixture to loosen it a little, before folding in the remainder with the tablespoon. Pour into a serving bowl, or into 4-6 glasses or individual dishes, and leave to set in the fridge overnight.

3 You can make the sauce a day in advance or a couple of hours before the meal. Put the sugar and water into a saucepan, add in the pepper and heat gently, stirring a little until the sugar has dissolved. Bring to the boil and boil for 5 minutes until slightly reduced. Add the strawberries and simmer over a low heat for 5 minutes.

4 Leave to cool slightly, then purée with a stick blender or in a blender. Taste and add extra finely and freshly ground pepper if you want more of a buzz. Leave to cool, cover and keep in the fridge until ready to serve. Serve poured on top of the mousse, or in a separate jug for pouring over as you like.

Lordahmercy! It might be just hot chocolate, but this is one of the best recipes in the book. I used to start the day off with hot chocolate when I was a child in Jamaica. Because of the rum I wouldn't suggest you have this version for breakfast – it would send you straight back to bed. But you'll sure sleep well if you have it at bedtime.

Serves 4–6

800ml (scant 1½ pints) milk

200ml (⅓ pint) double cream

115g (4oz) chocolate, broken into small pieces

3 tbsp soft dark brown sugar

1 cinnamon stick

1 vanilla pod

about ¼ tsp freshly grated nutmeg, or to taste

3 tbsp dark rum

To serve

400ml (14fl oz) double cream

2 tbsp soft dark brown sugar

cocoa powder, for sprinkling (optional)

4 cinnamon sticks or chocolate flakes (optional)

1 Put 200ml (⅓ pint) of the milk into a saucepan with the cream, chocolate, sugar and cinnamon stick. Slit the vanilla pod open lengthways with a sharp knife and scrape the little black seeds into the milk mixture using the handle of a teaspoon or the tip of the knife.

2 Heat the milk mixture gently, stirring to help the sugar dissolve and the chocolate to melt, until completely smooth. Add the remaining milk and bring to just under the boil. Turn the heat off, add the nutmeg and leave for 15 minutes or so to allow the flavours to meld.

3 Whip the cream for serving very lightly and then mix in the sugar with a large metal spoon.

4 Heat the chocolate milk again, right up to the boil, then add the rum. Remove the cinnamon stick and vanilla pod. Pour into cups or glass mugs and swirl the cream artily on top. If you like, sprinkle with cocoa powder and add a cinnamon stick or chocolate flake to each cup or mug. Serve immediately.

I love the way this cake tastes, with its fragrant spices coming through in a warm-flavoured syrup, and I love the way it looks with the spices on top. Have it for tea or for pud - especially if you're asking me round! Serve on its own or with vanilla or coconut ice cream, or cream.

Serves 8

160g (5¾oz) butter, softened, plus extra for greasing

70g (2½oz) light muscovado sugar

70g (2½oz) caster sugar

finely grated rind of 1 lime

1 tbsp dark rum

3 large eggs

100g (3½oz) ground almonds

85g (3oz) self-raising flour, sifted

For the spiced syrup

200ml (⅓ pint) water

40g (1½oz) granulated sugar

1 vanilla pod, cut in half crossways

½ chilli (ideally a red or yellow Scotch bonnet), with seeds

1 cinnamon stick, broken in half

4 cloves

2 bay leaves

2 tbsp dark rum (optional)

1 Preheat the oven to 140°C (fan)/160°C/gas mark 3. Lightly grease a 23cm (9in) round springform cake tin with butter.

2 Beat the butter and sugars together in a large mixing bowl until light and fluffy. Stir in the lime rind and rum. Stir in the eggs one at a time, alternating with a third of the ground almonds and a third of the flour. Transfer the mixture to the cake tin and bake for 35-45 minutes or until a skewer inserted into the centre of the cake comes out clean.

3 While the cake is baking, make the syrup. Put the water and sugar into a saucepan and heat gently, stirring a little, until the sugar has dissolved. Slit each vanilla half lengthways with a knife and scrape the little black seeds into the syrup using the handle of a teaspoon or the tip of the knife, then add the pods too. Add the chilli half, cinnamon halves, cloves and bay leaves and bring to the boil, then reduce the heat and simmer for 10 minutes so that the syrup thickens slightly and takes on the chilli heat and the fragrance of the spices. Turn the heat off and stir in the rum (if using).

4 Remove the cake from the oven and leave to cool slightly, then release it and leave to cool completely on a wire rack.

5 Set the cooled cake on a serving plate. Strain the spices from the syrup and reserve. Prick the cake all over with a fork and pour the syrup over slowly so that it is absorbed into the cake. Decorate the top of the cake with the reserved spices before serving.

These shortbread biscuits are just so tasty and moreish that you'll find they disappear in a flash! They can be stored in an airtight container and then heated up before serving.

Makes 18–20 shortbreads

100g (3½oz) plain flour, plus extra for dusting

½ tsp cayenne pepper

100g (3½oz) butter, diced, plus extra for greasing

50g (1¾oz) Parmesan cheese, freshly grated

50g (1¾oz) Cheddar cheese, grated

½–1 tbsp cold water

1 large egg yolk, beaten with a drop of water

18–20 pecan nut halves

1 Preheat the oven to 160°C (fan)/180°C/gas mark 4. Sift the flour with the cayenne pepper into a mixing bowl. Rub the butter into the dry ingredients with your fingertips and then stir in the cheeses. Use a knife and then your hands to mix in enough of the water to bring together into a ball. Wrap the dough in foil and leave to rest in the fridge for 30 minutes.

2 Roll the dough out on a lightly floured surface until about 8mm–1cm (⅜–½in) thick. Use a small biscuit cutter (about 6cm/2½in in diameter) to cut into small rounds. Put on a greased nonstick baking sheet. Brush the tops of the biscuits with the egg yolk and add a pecan half to the centre of each.

3 Bake for about 10 minutes or until browned. Leave to cool on the baking sheet for a couple of minutes, then carefully transfer to a wire rack and leave to cool. Serve warm or cold.

Please, please use a good-quality rum for this beautiful pud and let the fruit soak in it for a week. And make sure you have a lie down after you've eaten it!

Serves 10

125g (4½oz) mixed dried tropical fruit

100g (3½oz) mixed currants and raisins

125g (4½oz) dried figs

125g (4½oz) dried apples

50g (1¾oz) dried sour cherries

35g (1¼oz) chopped candied orange peel

1½ tsp ground cinnamon

1½ tsp ground ginger

1½ tsp freshly grated nutmeg

½ tsp ground allspice

grated rind and juice of 1 lemon and 1 orange

300ml (½ pint) white rum, plus extra for flaming (optional)

125g (4½oz) butter, softened, plus extra for greasing

150g (5½oz) soft light brown sugar

2 large eggs, lightly beaten

125g (4½oz) plain flour, sifted

½ tsp baking powder

pinch of salt

150g (5½oz) fresh white breadcrumbs

50g (1¾oz) mixed nuts, roughly chopped

3 tsp vanilla extract

1 Chop any large bits of the dried fruit into smaller chunks. Put all the dried fruit, candied peel, spices, citrus rind and juice and rum into a large bowl. Cover with clingfilm and leave to steep, at room temperature, for a week, stirring every day.

2 Grease a 1.7 litre (3 pint) pudding basin with butter. Beat the butter and sugar together in a large mixing bowl until light and fluffy. Beat in the eggs a little at a time, then stir in the flour, baking powder, salt, breadcrumbs, nuts and vanilla extract. Stir the fruit and all its soaking liquid into the pudding mixture and mix thoroughly. Spoon into the pudding basin.

3 Lay 2 large rectangles of greaseproof paper that will fit over the top of the pudding generously, and then a piece of foil the same size, on top of each other. Pleat them together across the middle. Use to cover the top of the pudding, with the pleat in the centre, and fold over the sides. Tie the cover tightly around the rim of the basin with kitchen string – you will need someone to help you. Make a string handle and attach to the sides so that you can easily lift the pudding in and out of the water as you steam it. Trim the foil and paper to leave about 5cm (2in) below the string.

4 Lower the pudding into a large saucepan with a trivet set on the base. Add enough boiling water to come halfway up the side of the basin. Cover with a lid and steam over a low heat (the water should always be simmering), adding more boiling water as necessary, for 6 hours. Leave to cool slightly, then remove the paper, foil and string. Cover the pudding as before. On Christmas Day, reheat the pudding by steaming again for 45–60 minutes. Turn it out on to a plate and decorate it with a sprig of holly. If you are brave, you can flame the pudding before you carry it to the table. Warm extra rum in a saucepan until only just beginning to boil, pour into a ladle and set alight with a match, then pour over the pudding – but beware of the flaming holly!

The macadamia is the meatiest of nuts as well as being delicious and this is a gorgeous and filling spicy snack to have with a nice cold glass of beer or ginger beer.

Serves 4–6 with drinks

150g (5½oz) macadamia nuts

1 tsp ground cumin

1 tsp ground coriander

1 tsp ground black pepper

good shake of cayenne pepper

¼–½ tsp sea salt

½ tbsp olive oil

1 Preheat the oven to 160°C (fan)/180°C/gas mark 4.

2 Spread the nuts out on a baking sheet and toast in the oven for about 10 minutes or until lightly browned, shaking them around once or twice.

3 Meanwhile, mix all the remaining ingredients together in a bowl.

4 Toss the toasted nuts in the spicy oil. Serve them warm or cold as nibbles.

BANANA, COCONUT & CINNAMON PANCAKES

These are like American or Scotch pancakes rather than the French version. They are lovely with honey or maple syrup poured over them and chopped pecans scattered on top.

Serves 6

115g (4oz) plain flour

4 tbsp soft light brown sugar

¼ tsp ground cinnamon

good pinch of salt

2 large eggs

300ml (½ pint) coconut milk

300ml (½ pint) water

3 very ripe bananas, peeled and mashed

25g (1oz) unsalted butter

1 Sift the flour into a bowl and stir in the sugar, cinnamon and salt. Beat the eggs lightly with the coconut milk and water and gradually add to the dry ingredients, stirring as you do so – there should be no lumps. Stir in the mashed banana.

2 Heat 15g (½oz) of the butter in a nonstick frying pan over a medium heat and spoon enough batter into the pan to make a 9cm (3½in) pancake. Cook 2 or 3 pancakes at a time, depending on the size of your pan. When you can see bubbles forming on the top, carefully flip the pancake over and cook on the other side until it is cooked all the way through. Cook the remaining batter in the same way, adding the remaining butter to the pan as necessary. Keep the cooked pancakes warm in a low oven and serve as soon as they are all ready.

This cake is a vision in white and perfect for a celebration. Instead of coconut you toast yourself, you can use sweetened shaved coconut if you can find it - healthfood stores sometimes stock it.

Serves 8–10

375g (13oz) unsalted butter, softened, plus extra for greasing

375g (13oz) caster sugar

6 large eggs, beaten

300ml (½ pint) coconut milk

375g (13oz) plain flour

finely grated rind and juice of 3 limes

2 tsp ground allspice

3 tsp baking powder

pinch of salt

100g (3½oz) desiccated coconut

For the buttercream

250g (9oz) unsalted butter, slightly softened

500g (1lb 2oz) icing sugar, sifted

finely grated rind and juice of 2 limes

To decorate

50g (1¾oz) fresh coconut flesh

1 tsp groundnut oil

1 Preheat the oven to 160°C (fan)/180°C/gas mark 4. Grease 3 x 22cm (8½in) cake tins with butter and line the bases with greaseproof paper.

2 Beat the butter and sugar together in a large mixing bowl until light and fluffy. Gradually beat in the eggs a little at a time. Fold in the coconut milk alternately with the flour using a large metal spoon. Add the lime rind and juice, allspice, baking powder and salt and mix until smooth, then stir in the desiccated coconut.

3 Divide the cake mixture between the prepared tins, spreading it level. Bake for 40 minutes or until a skewer inserted into the centre of the cakes comes out clean. Leave the cakes to cool for 5 minutes, then turn them out on to a wire rack, peel off the lining paper and leave to cool completely.

4 While the cake is cooling, make the buttercream. Beat the butter until light and fluffy in a bowl, then beat in the icing sugar a little at a time (to avoid clouds of icing sugar everywhere). Finally, beat in the lime rind and juice. Cover and leave in the fridge for 20 minutes to firm up a little.

5 Cut the coconut flesh into fine shavings using a small sharp knife. Heat the oil in a frying pan over a medium-high heat, add the coconut and cook, stirring frequently, until tinged with gold. Remove to a plate and leave to cool.

6 Put the first cake on a cake stand or serving plate and spread one-third of the buttercream over it. Place the second cake on top and spread with half the remaining buttercream. Cover with the final cake and spread the top with the remaining buttercream. Arrange the toasted coconut on top. The cake is ready to serve.

These macaroons look so great in a pile on a plate, and the texture is deliciously chewy. Use whatever you fancy to decorate them, but a red jam such as raspberry and an orange fruit such as mango make a good combination. Cardamom works brilliantly with coconut - just try it and see what I mean!

Makes 20

2 large egg whites

175g (6oz) caster sugar

50g (1¾oz) ground almonds

100g (3½oz) desiccated coconut

seeds from 6 cardamom seeds, crushed

1 tsp vanilla extract

To decorate

jam (such as raspberry)

ready-to-eat dried tropical fruit (such as mango)

1 Preheat the oven to 160°C (fan)/180°C/gas mark 4. Beat the egg whites with half the sugar in a bowl until soft peaks form, then beat in the remaining sugar. Stir in the ground almonds, coconut, cardamom and vanilla extract.

2 Line a nonstick baking sheet with baking paper. Place level dessertspoonfuls of the mixture in small, compact heaps on the baking sheet. On half the macaroons, make a small indentation in the top and carefully spoon in a small amount of jam. On the other half, place a small slither of ready-to-eat dried tropical fruit. Alternatively, you can really go to town and add jam AND fruit to them all – and a bit more jam at the end, after cooking, too!

3 Bake for about 15 minutes or until lightly browned. Leave to cool for 10 minutes on the baking sheet, then transfer to a wire rack and leave to cool completely.

I love trying different ways with my favourite ingredients. Grapefruit is very Caribbean and something I really enjoy - it wakes up your taste buds and makes you feel good. This is a new salad combination using fruit, and it looks and tastes great.

Serves 4 as a starter or side salad, or 2–3 as a light lunch

2 pink grapefruit

1 large avocado

100g (3½oz) rocket leaves

70g (2½oz) black olives, pitted and chopped

For the dressing

1 tsp clear honey

¼ tsp finely chopped deseeded red chilli (ideally Scotch bonnet)

1–1½ tbsp finely chopped mint

2–3 tbsp olive oil

very small pinch of salt

1 Using a very sharp knife, cut the rind and as much of the white pith as possible from the grapefruit. Holding each grapefruit in turn in one hand and ideally using a serrated knife, cut out each segment of fruit by slicing down between the flesh and the membrane, collecting any juice that comes out (you will need some for the dressing).

2 Halve, stone and peel the avocados, and then cut into medium-sized pieces. Mix with the grapefruit segments, rocket leaves and olives in a salad bowl.

3 To make the dressing, mix the honey with 1 tablespoon of the reserved grapefruit juice and stir until it has dissolved. Add the remaining ingredients and whisk hard to combine. Add the dressing to the salad, toss to coat and serve immediately.

With their Indian spicing, these pickled limes are seriously addictive. Treat them like you would a chutney or pickle – they're great with roast chicken or spicy lamb and rice dishes.

Makes about 500g (1lb 2oz)

500g (1lb 2oz) limes

50g (1¾oz) sea salt

1 tsp cardamom seeds

1 tsp cumin seeds

1 tsp allspice berries

½ tbsp chilli powder

250g (9oz) soft light brown sugar

4cm (1½in) piece of fresh root ginger, peeled and shredded

1 Put the limes into a bowl of cold water and leave them to soak overnight at room temperature.

2 Cut a small slice off the bottom and top of each lime, then cut into slices about 4mm (⅛in) thick. Put the lime slices into a glass or ceramic bowl with the salt and turn to coat well. Cover with a clean tea towel and leave to stand at room temperature overnight.

3 Use a blender or pestle and mortar to crush the whole spices, then mix with the chilli powder.

4 Drain the limes in a colander, catching the juices in a saucepan. Add the sugar to the juice and bring to the boil over a gentle heat, stirring a little to help the sugar dissolve. Stir in the spice mix and leave to cool.

5 Put the limes and ginger into 2 still-warm 250ml (9fl oz) sterilized preserving jars with glass or plastic (acid or vinegar-proof) lids (*see* page 106 for sterilizing instructions) and pour over the sweet syrup. Seal. Leave in a warm place for about 5 days before storing in a cool, dark place, and consume within a year. You can eat the limes after a month. Once opened, refrigerate and use within 3 months, making sure that the pickles are always covered in syrup (if they are not, add more lime juice to the jar to top up).

It's hard to work out exactly what flavours are in some dishes, and this is sure to fox your guests, who won't expect to find thyme in an ice cream. Boozy and subtle, this is definitely one for the adults.

Serves 8

570ml (19fl oz) double cream

2 sprigs of thyme

2 strips of orange rind

125g (4½oz) caster sugar

275ml (scant ½ pint) freshly squeezed orange juice

125ml (4fl oz) curaçao

1 Heat the cream, thyme sprigs, orange rind and sugar in a saucepan until boiling, stirring a little to help the sugar dissolve. Once boiling point is reached, turn the heat off and leave to infuse.

2 Strain the infused cream into a bowl to remove the thyme sprigs and orange rind. Stir in the orange juice and curaçao, cover and leave to chill in the fridge.

3 Pour the chilled mixture into an ice cream machine and churn according to the manufacturer's instructions. If you don't have an ice cream machine, pour the mixture into a shallow freezer-proof container – preferably metal, as that conducts the coldness well – and put it into the coldest part of your freezer for about 6–7 hours until firm. Beat the ice cream with a fork or an electric whisk about 5 times during the freezing process to ensure a smooth, creamy finish. Serve in scoops in individual dishes or glasses.

These lovely little marmalade puddings are perfect for the end of a posh supper or Sunday lunch, as they are baked in individual portions. Cardamom is just the business with citrus flavours, but don't use it too much – it needs to be handled with care. Serve with whipped cream or vanilla ice cream.

Serves 8

175g (6oz) butter, softened, plus extra for greasing and 8 knobs for the moulds

175g (6oz) soft light brown sugar

3 large eggs

175g (6oz) self-raising flour

seeds from 12 cardamom pods, crushed

1 tsp vanilla extract

finely grated rind of 2 oranges

3 tbsp milk

16 tbsp orange marmalade

For the syrup

6 tbsp orange marmalade

2 tbsp soft light brown sugar

15g (½oz) unsalted butter

juice of 4 oranges

seeds from 4 cardamom pods, ground

1 Preheat the oven to 160°C (fan)/180°C/gas mark 4. Grease 8 small pudding moulds really well with butter.

2 Beat the butter and sugar together in a large mixing bowl until light and fluffy. Gradually beat in the eggs a little at a time. Fold in the flour, cardamom, vanilla extract, orange rind and milk with a large metal spoon.

3 Put a knob of butter into each pudding mould and then 2 tablespoons marmalade. Pour the pudding mixture on top, dividing it evenly between the moulds and leaving room for the puddings to rise.

4 Bake for about 20 minutes or until a skewer inserted into the centre of the puddings comes out clean. They will be very hot, so it is fine to leave them to cool while you make the syrup.

5 Put all ingredients for the syrup into a saucepan and bring to the boil over a gentle heat. Stir and then boil for 2 minutes to reduce. Turn the heat off.

6 Run a knife around each pudding to help loosen it. Invert the puddings on to individual plates. Pour the warm syrup slowly over each one and serve immediately.

Mmmmmmmmmmmmmm! This really is a great dessert. Allspice gives the oranges quite a different, distinctive taste, and rosemary works surprisingly well with sweet dishes. Serve with cream if you prefer.

Serves 4

4 large seedless oranges

ice cream, to serve

For the allspice and rosemary caramel sauce

100ml (3½fl oz) water

150g (5½oz) granulated sugar

juice of 1 large orange

1 tsp allspice berries

3 sprigs of rosemary, plus extra to garnish

1 First make the caramel sauce. Put the water and sugar into a heavy-based saucepan and heat gently to dissolve the sugar, which it should do without the liquid boiling. Don't stir it at first, but when halfway to dissolving, carefully run a spoon through any undissolved sugar on the bottom of the pan to help it along. When all the sugar has dissolved, increase the heat and boil until it is dark brown. Watch it carefully – it can go from dark brown to burnt in an instant. Add the orange juice just at the point when it is really brown – take care, as it will spit. Turn the heat off, stir in the allspice and rosemary and leave to cool.

2 Using a very sharp knife, cut the rind and as much of the white pith as possible from the oranges. Cut into thin slices and put into a serving dish. Add any juice that comes out to the caramel sauce, which will have thickened in the process of cooling. Remove the allspice berries if you like, or leave them in for your guests to discard (they should not eat them). Pour over the cold caramel sauce, cover and leave to chill in the fridge.

3 Serve the orange slices decorated with extra rosemary sprigs, with a scoop of ice cream alongside.

This is the sort of pudding my mum made for me when I first arrived in the UK and now I've given it my own spiced-up twist. The combination of cinnamon and nutmeg with the orange makes it special. This is one for you, Mum.

Serves 6

For the pastry

100g (3½oz) butter, chilled and diced

180g (6¼oz) plain flour, sifted, plus extra for dusting

pinch of salt

1 tsp caster sugar

about 2 tbsp cold water

For the filling

30g (1oz) cornflour

300ml (½ pint) freshly squeezed orange juice (7–8 juicing oranges)

75g (2¾oz) light muscovado sugar

2 large egg yolks

1½ tbsp finely grated orange rind

1½ tsp ground cinnamon

½ tsp freshly grated nutmeg

For the meringue

2 large egg whites

50g (1¾oz) light muscovado sugar

50g (1¾oz) caster sugar

cream, to serve

1 First make the pastry. Put all the ingredients, except the water, into a food processor and whizz using the pulse button until it has the texture of breadcrumbs. Add enough of the water to bring it together into a ball as you briefly mix it. If making it by hand, mix the flour and salt together in a bowl, rub in the butter with your fingertips until it has the texture of breadcrumbs, then stir in the sugar. Use a knife and then your hands to mix in enough of the water to bring it together into a ball.

2 Roll the dough out on a lightly floured work surface and use it to line a 20cm (8in) tart tin. Leave it to rest in the fridge for 30 minutes.

3 Preheat the oven to 160°C (fan)/180°C/gas mark 4. Put a sheet of foil into the tart case and fill with baking beans or rice. Bake the tart case for 15 minutes. Remove the beans or rice and foil and bake for another 10 minutes until lightly brown. Remove from the oven and reduce the oven temperature to 130°C (fan)/150°C/gas mark 2.

4 While the pastry is baking, make the orange custard filling. Mix the cornflour with 2 tablespoons of the orange juice in a bowl. Put the remaining orange juice and sugar into a saucepan and heat gently, stirring a little, until the sugar has dissolved. Pour on to the cornflour mixture, stirring as you do so. Return the mixture to the pan and boil, stirring constantly, for about 3 minutes or until it has thickened. Leave to cool for a minute or so, then whisk in the egg yolks, orange rind, cinnamon and nutmeg. Pour into the tart case in an even layer.

5 To make the meringue, whisk the egg whites in a bowl until stiff. Gradually whisk in the muscovado sugar and then the caster sugar a little at a time. Dollop the meringue on top of the filling, covering it completely. Bake in the oven for 30 minutes or until the meringue is lightly brown. Serve with cream.

I grew up with limeade in Jamaica, but in Britain I'm now also into lemons and this is a refreshing drink given a sophisticated edge with the addition of vanilla. A real thirst quencher, this is also the business when you add rum!

Serves 4

6 unwaxed lemons

150g (5½oz) caster sugar

1.5 litres (2¾ pints) just-boiled water

½ vanilla pod (best to use one that has been cut open and had its seeds used in another recipe)

To serve (optional)

ice cubes

rum, gin or vodka and tonic water

1 Carefully pare the rind from 3 lemons, trying to avoid including any of the bitter white pith (a good peeler works well, or use a sharp knife).

2 Squeeze out the juice from all the lemons and put into a glass or ceramic bowl along with the rind and the sugar. Pour over the water, add the vanilla pod half and give it all a good stir. Cover with clingfilm and leave in a cool place overnight.

3 Give the lemonade another good stir, then strain off the rind and vanilla pod half (you can wash and dry it and use again, or add it to a jar of sugar to give it a lovely scent). Cover and leave to chill in the fridge.

4 Serve over ice cubes, straight up or slightly diluted with water, or with rum, gin or vodka and some tonic water if you want to booze it up as well as spice it up!

11

Here's a fresh-tasting sour-sweet salad that is very good served as a cooler with a hot main course. To vary it, you can also add some sliced sweet cherry tomatoes – try yellow ones, if you can get them.

Serves 4 as a side dish

½ melon

½ large cucumber

1 mango

For the dressing

1 tbsp white wine vinegar

2 tbsp groundnut oil

3 tbsp olive oil

20 mint leaves

1 red chilli, deseeded and shredded, plus extra to garnish (if brave enough!)

2 tsp caster sugar

salt and black pepper

1 First make the dressing. Put all the dressing ingredients into a blender and whizz using the pulse button until thoroughly blended.

2 Remove the seeds from the melon. Cut the fruit into wedges, then slice the flesh away from the skin of each wedge and cut into cubes about 2.5cm (1in) in size.

3 How you deal with the cucumber skin is up to you. I like to partially peel the skin so that I am left with a stripy cucumber, but some people find the skin indigestible, so do it your way. Cut the cucumber in half lengthways and then scoop the seeds out of each half with a teaspoon. Cut each half into slices about 3mm (⅛in) thick.

4 Peel the mango, then cut off the 'cheeks' by slicing through the flesh either side of the central stone so that you have 2 rounded fleshy sides and a stone with quite a lot of fruit round it. Cut as much of the fruit from around the stone as you can, then cut all the flesh into cubes about 2.5cm (1in) in size.

5 Toss the melon, cucumber and mango together with the dressing. Serve garnished with extra shreds of chilli, if you dare, but with a warning that these will be super hot!

This is what I'd cook if you were coming round to my gaff. Pineapple is a symbol of hospitality and the star of this dish, with a subtle spicing of bay leaves and allspice berries. Serve this on its own, or with cream or coconut ice cream.

Serves 4–6

1 pineapple

2 mangoes

For the bay, allspice and lime syrup

100ml (3½fl oz) water

100g (3½oz) caster sugar

4 bay leaves

14 allspice berries

1 lime

100ml (3½fl oz) rum (optional)

1 First make the syrup. Put the water, sugar, bay leaves and allspice into a small saucepan. Finely grate the rind from the lime and add to the pan. Heat gently, stirring a little, until the sugar has dissolved. Leave to simmer on the lowest heat for 15 minutes to thicken slightly and allow the flavours of the spices and lime rind to infuse the syrup. Squeeze out the lime juice and add to the syrup. Leave to cool.

2 Using a very sharp knife, cut the skin from the pineapple, removing any remaining 'eyes'. Cut downwards into quarters. Remove the hard central core from each quarter and then cut each piece into 4 long strips and then each of these strips in half.

3 Peel the mango, then cut off the 'cheeks' by slicing through the flesh either side of the central stone so that you have 2 rounded fleshy sides and a stone with quite a lot of fruit round it. Cut as much of the fruit from around the stone as you can, then cut all the flesh into chunks about 3cm (1¼in) in size.

4 Put all the fruit into a serving bowl. If you want a simpler but slightly less tasty and attractive dish, pour the cooled syrup into the bowl through a colander so that you catch the allspice berries and bay leaves. You can then put the bay leaves back, if you like, but discard the berries. Otherwise, pour everything over and let your guests remove the spices. Mix the fruit with the syrup.

5 For the best flavour, cover and leave to infuse in a cool place or in the fridge for 30 minutes (although you can make it a couple of hours in advance if you prefer). When you come to serve the fruits, if you have left the allspice berries in, you can invite your guests to suck on them as they go and then leave them on the side of the plate, if they like. Unlike peppercorns, they won't bite!

My Mango & Cucumber Relish is good served with the Rum, Chilli and Brown Sugar Cured Salmon on page 48. Try my Mango & Coconut Relish with my Hot, Hot Roots (see page 92).

Serves 8

2 just-ripe mangoes

1 small cucumber

½ small red onion, finely chopped

2 red chillies, deseeded and shredded

juice of 1 lime

2 tbsp olive oil

2 garlic cloves, very finely chopped

3 tbsp chopped fresh coriander

2 spring onions, finely chopped

salt and black pepper

a little caster sugar (optional)

1 Peel each mango, then cut off the 'cheeks' by slicing through the flesh either side of the central stone so that you have 2 rounded fleshy sides and a stone with quite a lot of fruit round it. Cut as much of the fruit from around the stone as you can, then cut all the flesh into cubes about 1cm (½in) in size.

2 Cut the cucumber in half lengthways and then scoop the seeds out of each half with a teaspoon. Chop each half into cubes about 5mm (¼in) in size.

3 Mix the mango and cucumber with all the remaining ingredients in a serving dish, adjust the seasoning to taste and serve.

MANGO & COCONUT RELISH

For the relish

75g (2¾oz) desiccated coconut

2 just-ripe mangoes

½ tsp black mustard seeds

2 tsp caster sugar

good pinch of salt

½ tbsp dark rum

juice of 2 limes

2 red chillies, deseeded and very finely sliced

1 generous handful of mint leaves

1 Put the coconut into a heatproof bowl and add enough boiling water to just cover. Leave for about 30 minutes until the water has been absorbed.

2 Peel the mangoes, then cut off the 'cheeks' by slicing through the flesh either side of the central stone so that you have 2 rounded fleshy sides and a stone with quite a lot of fruit round it. Slice the 'cheeks' lengthways into slender wedges. Slice as much of the fruit from around the stone as you can, trying to keep the wedges long and elegant.

3 Put the soaked coconut, mustard seeds, sugar, salt and rum into a blender and whizz to make a coarse paste. Layer up the mango wedges with spoonfuls of the coconut paste, squeezing on the lime juice as you go and sprinkling with the chilli and mint.

Try to put out of your mind all those haunting memories of horrible tapioca pudding served up at school. This is a strictly sophisticated dish and also a good one to prepare ahead when cooking for friends.

Serves 6

400ml can coconut milk

200ml (1/3 pint) milk

1/2 cinnamon stick

60g (2¼oz) caster sugar, plus extra for the brûlée

60g (2¼oz) tapioca

2 limes

100ml (3½fl oz) double cream

2 large, just-ripe mangoes

4 passion fruit

icing sugar, for dusting

1 Heat the coconut milk, milk and cinnamon in a saucepan until just boiling. Reduce the heat and add the caster sugar and tapioca, stirring as you do so to help the sugar dissolve and prevent the tapioca from forming lumps. Cook the tapioca over a low heat, stirring occasionally, for about 30 minutes or until the pearls are transparent and softened. Pour the mixture into a bowl and leave to cool.

2 Meanwhile, remove the rind from the limes with a zester, cover and set aside for decorating. Squeeze the juice from one of the limes. Lightly whip the cream.

3 When the tapioca is cold, stir in the lime juice and fold in the cream with a large metal spoon.

4 Peel the mangoes, then cut off the 'cheeks' by slicing through the flesh either side of the central stone so that you have 2 rounded fleshy sides and a stone with quite a lot of fruit round it. Cut as much of the fruit from around the stone as you can, then cut all the flesh into slices. Reserve several slices to decorate the puddings, then put the remaining mango into a bowl.

5 Preheat the grill to high. Using a teaspoon, scrape the juice and seeds from the passion fruit on to the mango. Distribute the fruit between 6 ramekin dishes, cover with the tapioca and spoon an even, thin layer of caster sugar on top. Set the ramekins in the grill pan, put under the grill and heat until the sugar topping has caramelized. (Alternatively, use a cook's blowtorch to caramelize the topping.) Leave the sugar to harden at room temperature – if you refrigerate the puddings once they have been brûléed, it will make the topping soggy.

6 Cut the reserved mango slices into fine slivers. Sift a little icing sugar on to the top of each ramekin and decorate with the slivers of mango and the lime rind.

This fabulocious sorbet has a chilli kick, making it hot-hot and cool-cool all at the same time. Lordahmercy!

Serves 8–10

3 mangoes (about 800g/1lb 12oz total weight)

about 225ml (8fl oz) sugar syrup (*see* below)

1 tbsp lime juice

¼–¾ red chilli, deseeded and finely chopped

1 large egg white, beaten

For the sugar syrup

150ml (¼ pint) water

150g (5½oz) granulated sugar

1 First make the sugar syrup. Put the water and sugar into a saucepan and heat gently, stirring a little, until the sugar has dissolved. Increase the heat and simmer for 5 minutes.

2 Peel the mangoes, then cut off the 'cheeks' by slicing through the flesh either side of the central stone so that you have 2 rounded fleshy sides and a stone with quite a lot of fruit round it. Cut as much of the fruit from around the stone as you can. Put all the flesh into a blender and whizz until smooth.

3 Measure how much mango purée you have and mix with half that quantity of sugar syrup. Stir in the lime juice and chilli. Cover and leave to chill in fridge.

4 Pour the chilled mixture into in an ice cream machine and churn until the mixture is nearly firm. While the machine is still running, add the beaten egg white and then continue to churn until firm, according to the manufacturer's instructions. Store in the freezer until ready to serve. (If you don't have an ice cream machine, pour the mixture into a shallow freezer-proof container – preferably metal, as it conducts the coldness well – and put it in the coldest part of the freezer for about 6 hours until nearly firm. Remove it from the freezer 3 or 4 times during the freezing process and whizz it briefly in a food processor – letting it refreeze almost entirely each time – for a smoother texture. After this, stir in the beaten egg white and then return the sorbet to the freezer for another 1-2 hours until firm, stirring it up once more during the process. Store in the freezer until ready to serve.)

5 Transfer to the fridge for 15 minutes or so to soften a little before serving. Serve in small dishes, glasses or even teacups.

Pineapple and cinnamon is an unusual and successful combination, but then made into a crumble it becomes even more magical! Try it with my Nutmeg Coconut Custard (see page 65) for a special treat, or simply serve with cream.

Serves 6

1 pineapple, peeled, cored and cut into 3cm (1¼in) chunks

1 tbsp light muscovado sugar

2 tsp ground cinnamon

Nutmeg Coconut Custard (*see* page 65), to serve

For the crumble topping

150g (5½oz) plain flour, sifted

salt

150g (5½oz) butter, chilled and diced

25g (1oz) desiccated coconut

100g (3½oz) light muscovado sugar

1 Heat the oven to 180°C (fan)/200°C/gas mark 6. First make the crumble topping. Put all the ingredients into a food processor and whizz using the pulse button until it has the texture of breadcrumbs. If making by hand, mix the flour and salt together in a bowl, rub in the butter with your fingertips until it has the texture of breadcrumbs, then stir in the coconut and sugar.

2 Put the pineapple into an ovenproof dish, sprinkle with the sugar and cinnamon and mix well. Spoon the crumble mixture on top in an even layer.

3 Set the dish on a baking sheet and bake in the oven for 25 minutes or until lightly brown on top. Serve with my Nutmeg and Coconut Custard.

This is obviously a dessert, but I have eaten the granita on its own, at any time of day, as it's so thirst quenching. This is particularly good for people who are trying to lose a bit of weight, as there isn't too much sugar in it and no fat at all.

Serves

400ml (14fl oz) water

350g (12oz) granulated sugar

5 fine strips of lime rind

juice of 6 limes

2 pineapples

For the granita

750ml (1⅓ pints) water

250g (9oz) granulated sugar

75g (2¾oz) fresh root ginger, peeled and grated

finely grated rind of 1 lime

juice of 6 limes

1 To make the syrup for the pineapple, put the water and sugar into a saucepan and heat gently, stirring a little, until the sugar has dissolved. Add the lime rind strips, bring to the boil and simmer for 5 minutes. Turn the heat off, stir in the lime juice and leave to cool completely. Remove the lime rind.

2 If you like, using a very sharp knife, cut the skin from each pineapple, removing any remaining 'eyes' (otherwise you can leave the skin on). Cut into large wedges and remove the hard central core from each wedge. Put the pineapple into a bowl and pour over the cold lime syrup. Cover and leave in the fridge until you need it.

3 To make the sugar syrup for the granita, heat the water and sugar as before, but this time just bring the water up to the boil – there is no need to keep simmering it. Turn the heat off, then add the ginger and grated lime rind. Cover and leave to infuse, at room temperature, overnight.

4 Strain the infused syrup and stir in the lime juice. Pour into a shallow freezer-proof container and freeze for 4–5 hours until firm. Use a fork to roughly break up the crystals 4 or 5 times during the freezing process.

5 To serve, pile the granita into glasses and insert 2 wedges of the pineapple at angles, skin-side up, in each glass.

VANILLA BANANA SPLIT
WITH PECAN PRALINE

How could anyone resist a banana split? And it's even better with my special pecan praline sprinkled on top and extra caramel from the dulce de leche - an Argentinian caramel sauce that you'll find in good supermarkets. Vanilla flavours both the ice cream and the cream here.

Serves 4

150ml (¼ pint) whipping cream

½ tsp vanilla extract

4 bananas, peeled and diagonally sliced

12 small scoops vanilla ice cream

6–8 tbsp *dulce de leche*

For the pecan praline

sunflower oil, for oiling

50g (1¾oz) pecan nuts

50g (1¾oz) caster sugar

1 First make the praline. Brush a baking sheet lightly with oil. Put the pecans and sugar into a heavy-based saucepan and heat gently. As the sugar melts and starts to brown, stir it with a metal spoon. When really brown (this takes just a few minutes), pour on to the oiled baking sheet. Leave to cool and then roughly break up with the end of a rolling pin so that you can see pieces of pecan.

2 Whip the cream until it holds peaks, then stir in the vanilla extract.

3 To assemble, in 4 glass tumblers layer up the banana slices, praline, ice cream and drizzles of the *dulce de leche*, then top with the cream, a little more praline and a final drizzle of *dulce de leche*. Grab a spoon and get stuck in!

12

This is named after Blue Mountain coffee, which comes from Jamaica and is one of the most famous (and expensive) coffees in the world. Coffee tastes great with spices and particularly with cardamom, cinnamon and vanilla - so they're all in this.

Serves 4–5

2–3 tbsp ground coffee

100ml (3½fl oz) just-boiled water

300ml (½ pint) double cream

seeds from 8 cardamom pods, roughly crushed

10cm (4in) piece of cinnamon stick, broken in half

4 large egg yolks

1 tbsp light muscovado sugar

½ tsp vanilla extract

4 tbsp caster sugar

1 First make some very strong coffee. Put the ground coffee with the water into a cafetière, leave to infuse for 4 minutes and then plunge. Put the cream, coffee, cardamom and cinnamon pieces into a small saucepan. Heat slowly until nearly boiling, then turn the heat off and leave to infuse for 30 minutes.

2 Preheat the oven to 170°C (fan)/190°C/gas mark 5. Whisk the egg yolks and muscovado sugar together in a bowl and pour on the infused cream, straining it through a sieve to remove most of the cardamom and the cinnamon pieces. Quickly wash and dry the pan.

3 Whisk the spicy coffee cream into the egg yolk mixture and return to the cleaned pan. Cook, stirring constantly, over a very gentle heat until slightly thickened. Add the vanilla extract.

4 Pour into a small ovenproof dish or 4 ramekins. Stand in a roasting tin and pour boiling water from a kettle into the tin so that it comes to halfway up the dish or ramekins. Bake for 10-15 minutes, if using one dish, or 5-10 minutes if using ramekins or until just set with a slight wobble in the centre. Remove from the oven and leave to cool. Cover and leave to chill in the fridge for at least 4 hours.

5 Preheat the grill to high. Spoon the caster sugar evenly on top of the custard, put under the grill (set the ramekins on a baking sheet) and heat until the sugar topping has caramelized. Alternatively, use a cook's blowtorch to caramelize the topping. Leave the sugar to harden at room temperature and then serve.

This is a great dessert to have at a party - it's rich, spicy, intense and special. You can vary the spicing to your taste, but this is how I like it. Serve it either warm or cold, with cream or ice cream.

Serves 8–10

150g (5½oz) plain flour, sifted, plus extra for dusting

pinch of salt

1 tsp ground cinnamon

75g (2¾oz) butter, chilled and diced

1 large egg yolk, beaten with 1 tbsp cold water

vanilla ice cream, to serve

For the filling

300g (10½oz) plain dark chocolate, broken into pieces, plus extra, grated, to decorate

3 tsp instant coffee granules, dissolved in 1 tbsp hot water

60g (2¼oz) soft dark brown sugar

3 large egg yolks plus 2 large eggs

finely grated rind of ½ large orange

1 tsp ground cinnamon

seeds from 3 cardamom pods, crushed

200ml (⅓ pint) double cream

2 tbsp dark rum

1 First make the pastry. Mix the flour, salt and cinnamon together in a bowl. Rub in the butter with your fingertips until it is the texture of breadcrumbs. Use a knife and then your hands to mix in the egg yolk and water and bring the mixture together in a ball. Wrap in foil and leave to chill in the fridge for 30 minutes.

2 Roll the dough out on a lightly floured work surface and use to line a 23cm (9in) tart tin. Leave to rest in the fridge for 30 minutes.

3 Preheat the oven to 160°C (fan)/180°C/gas mark 4. Put a sheet of foil into the tart case and fill with baking beans or rice. Bake the tart case for 20 minutes. Remove the beans or rice and foil and bake for another 5 minutes. Remove from the oven, leaving the oven on.

4 Meanwhile make the filling. Put the chocolate into a heatproof bowl set over a saucepan of barely simmering water, making sure that the bottom of the bowl does not touch the water, and leave until melted, stirring occasionally to help it along. Mix in the coffee and sugar, stirring until the sugar has dissolved. Remove the bowl from the pan and stir in all the remaining ingredients.

5 Pour the filling into the tart case and bake in the oven for 15 minutes. Leave to cool. Serve with a scoop of vanilla ice cream, sprinkled with grated chocolate.

I stole this idea from Italy - I hope the Italians don't mind - because it's super thirst-quenching. But adding a touch of spice and rum has given it a Caribbean edge.

Serves 6

60g (2¼oz) ground coffee

675ml (scant 1¼ pints) water

175g (6oz) caster sugar

seeds from 12 cardamom pods, crushed

To serve

300ml (½ pint) whipping cream

icing sugar, to taste

rum, to taste

1 Put the coffee into a saucepan with the water, sugar and cardamom. Bring to the boil, stirring a little to help the sugar dissolve, then turn the heat off and leave to stand until lukewarm. Strain through a coffee filter paper or a sieve lined with muslin into a glass or ceramic bowl. Leave to cool, then cover and leave to chill in the fridge.

2 Pour the mixture into a shallow freezer-proof container and freeze for 4-5 hours until firm. Use a fork to roughly break up the crystals 4-5 times during the freezing process.

3 Whip the cream until it holds peaks and then sweeten with icing sugar to taste. Fold in rum to taste with a large metal spoon.

4 Spoon the granita into glass tumblers and burrow down into the centre of each serving to make a little tunnel. Spoon the cream into the tunnel, finishing with a swirl on top, and serve immediately.

You can use any kind of coffee with this, just so long as it's strong! I like Jamaican coffee. This is a real knockout Caribbean version of Irish coffee. The spiced rum is so good that I like to drink a tot on its own.

Serves 4–6

100ml (3½fl oz) dark rum

4 strips of unwaxed orange rind

1 vanilla pod, split open lengthways

1 long cinnamon stick, broken in half

2 tbsp ground coffee (ideally Blue Mountain)

250ml (9fl oz) just-boiled water

4 tsp light muscovado sugar

double cream, for topping

1 Put the rum into a small saucepan with the orange rind, vanilla pod and cinnamon halves. Heat gently for a minute, then turn the heat off and leave to infuse for an hour or longer until you are ready to make the coffee.

2 Strain off the rind and spices and put them into a cafetière with the coffee. Pour over the water and leave to infuse for 5 minutes. Plunge the cafetière and pour the spiced coffee into small glasses or cups. Stir in as much of the rum as you like – saving the rest for another time – and then stir 1 teaspoon sugar into each cup. Pour cream over the back of a teaspoon to float on top.

Strange as it sounds, cold tea is a classic ingredient for a rum punch. This one uses the fragrance of jasmine tea with the subtle taste of cinnamon and a little bit of ginger to spice it up, plus the fruitiness of passion fruit and the kick of rum.

Makes 1 jug for 4–8, depending on your friends!

2 tsp loose-leaf jasmine tea or 1 jasmine teabag

2 cinnamon sticks, broken in half

400ml (14fl oz) warm water (2 parts just-boiled to 1 part cold)

juice of 2 limes

300ml (½ pint) passion fruit juice

200ml (⅓ pint) rum (optional)

3 tbsp stem ginger syrup

3–5 tsp soft light brown sugar, to taste

To serve

ice cubes or crushed ice

slices of lime

1 First make the tea. Put the loose-leaf tea or teabag into a teapot with the cinnamon halves and pour on the water. (Do not make the tea with only boiling water or it will be bitter.) Leave to infuse for 5 minutes, then strain into a jug, add the cinnamon halves and leave to cool.

2 When the tea is cool, add the lime juice, passion fruit juice and rum (if using). Add the ginger syrup and then the sugar to taste, stirring a little until it has dissolved. Cover and leave to chill in the fridge.

3 Serve the tea punch over ice cubes or crushed ice with a lime slice added to each glass. If you like, use a cinnamon half as a spicy swizzle stick, one for each glass if serving 4 people.

I love tea. In my house it's tea, tea, tea - it's a Brit thing. In the Caribbean, tea is more of a once-a-day drink, but for me it's all day, and not just when it's cold. I'm one of those guys who thinks that drinking tea cools you down. Chai is an Indian tea, sweet and spicy, and yet another way to enjoy this wonderful drink. It's believed to help ward off colds, too.

Serves 4

¼ tsp freshly grated nutmeg

about 3cm (1¼in) piece of fresh root ginger, peeled and sliced

½ cinnamon stick

5 cloves

1 star anise

2 drops of vanilla extract

200ml (⅓ pint) milk

400ml (14fl oz) water

4 tsp caster sugar

2 tsp black loose-leaf tea

1 Mix all the spices together, except the vanilla extract. Put the spices with all the remaining ingredients, including the vanilla, into a small saucepan.

2 Bring to the boil, then reduce the heat and simmer for 3 minutes. Strain into cups and serve immediately.

This isn't alcoholic, but you kind of think it is as you sip it, so it's a great summer drink if you're trying not to get too tipsy and yet still have a good time.

Makes about 2.5 litres (4½ pints)

600ml (1 pint) freshly brewed black tea (without milk)

3cm (1¼in) piece of fresh root ginger, peeled and finely sliced

600ml (1 pint) orange juice

300ml (½ a) pineapple juice

1.2 litres (2 pints) ginger ale

juice of 3 limes

2 tbsp caster sugar

1 handful of mint leaves

To serve

ice cubes

fruit of your choice, such as chopped pineapple and slices of orange

1 Put the tea into a saucepan and add the ginger. Bring to the boil, then reduce the heat and simmer for about 5 minutes. Leave until completely cold and then strain.

2 Mix the gingery tea with all the remaining ingredients. Pour into a jug full of ice cubes, add any fruit you might like – chopped pineapple and slices of orange work particularly well – and serve.

13

Nutmeg is a flavour that Caribbean people love and use a lot of, and this cake really shows it off well. It's a treat for afternoon tea (though I'd still serve it with some cream) or delicious as a dessert.

Serves 8–10

125g (4½oz) butter, softened, plus extra for greasing

125g (4½oz) soft light brown sugar

2 large eggs, lightly beaten

1 tsp vanilla extract

175g (6oz) plain flour

1½ tsp baking powder

pinch of salt

about ¼ nutmeg, freshly grated

4 tbsp milk

For the rum syrup

75ml (2½fl oz) water

75ml (2½fl oz) soft dark brown sugar

6 tbsp dark rum

1 Preheat the oven to 160°C (fan)/180°C/gas mark 4. Grease a 27 × 12.5cm (10¾ × 4¾in) loaf tin with butter and line the base with greaseproof paper.

2 Beat the butter and sugar together in a large mixing bowl until light and fluffy. Beat in the eggs a little at a time. If the mixture starts to curdle, mix in a tablespoon of the flour. Stir in the vanilla extract, then sift the flour, baking powder, salt and nutmeg together and fold into the mixture using a large metal spoon. Finally, stir in the milk.

3 Spoon the cake mixture into the prepared tin and bake in the oven for 45 minutes or until a skewer inserted into the centre of the cake comes out clean.

4 While the cake is baking, make the rum syrup. Put the water and sugar into a saucepan and bring to the boil over a gentle heat, stirring a little to help the sugar dissolve. Boil for 2 minutes. Add the rum and leave to cool.

5 When the cooked cake is still warm, pierce it all over with a skewer and slowly pour the rum syrup over it (if you work slowly, you will be able to pour more of it into the holes you have pierced). Leave the soaked cake to cool in the tin, then carefully remove it and put it into a cake tin (or wrap in foil). It is best eaten the next day, once it has had time to really soak up the rum syrup.

A 'Dark and Stormy' is a classic Caribbean cocktail made with ginger beer, dark rum and a slice of lime. This sorbet is more of a 'light and stormy', as the colour is paler once the liquid has been frozen. The handmade version has a more granular, granita-like texture than the version you'll get with an ice-cream machine, but it's equally delicious.

Serves 6

100ml (3½fl oz) water

100g (3½oz) granulated sugar

1 tsp grated lime rind

juice of 2 limes

75ml (2½fl oz) dark rum

250ml (9fl oz) ginger beer

1 Put the water and sugar into a small saucepan and heat gently, stirring a little, until the sugar has dissolved. Bring to the boil and boil for 2 minutes to reduce the liquid slightly to make a sugar syrup. Leave to cool.

2 Pour the sugar syrup into a jug and mix with the lime rind and juice, rum and ginger beer. Cover and leave to chill in the fridge.

3 Pour the chilled mixture into in an ice cream machine and churn until the mixture is firm, according to the manufacturer's instructions. Store in the freezer until ready to serve. (If you don't have an ice cream machine, pour the mixture into a shallow freezer-proof container – preferably metal, as it conducts the coldness well – and put it in the coldest part of the freezer overnight until firm. The following day, remove the sorbet from the freezer and whizz it briefly in a food processor. Return it to the freezer for another 3 hours, letting it refreeze almost entirely, then remove and whizz it again. Return the sorbet to the freezer for at least another 3 hours and then store there until ready to serve.)

4 Transfer to the fridge for 15 minutes or so to soften a little before serving. Spoon it into small bowls or glasses – this is boozy!

This is like a hot toddy and I certainly enjoy it at bedtime... Vary the spices according to your tastes - and then you can try it out lots and lots of times.

Serves 6–8

30g (1oz) unsalted butter

4–6 tbsp light muscovado sugar

300ml (½ pint) dark rum

300ml (½ pint) freshly squeezed orange juice (7–8 juicing oranges)

300ml (½ pint) water

½ tsp freshly grated nutmeg, plus extra to serve (optional)

½ cinnamon stick

4 cloves

1 Put all the ingredients into a saucepan. Heat gently, stirring, until the butter has melted and the sugar has dissolved completely.

2 Strain the mixture into small cups. Sprinkle the tops with a little extra nutmeg, if you like, before serving.

Get ready – this is going to blast your head off! You don't need to go to the ends of the earth for any unusual ingredients if you can't find curaçao, use Cointreau instead, but after drinking a couple of glasses you'll be lying on a beach on the other side of the world. Make a huge jugful and invite your mates round. You can add chunks of fresh mango or pineapple, too, if you want.

Serves as many as you want to treat!

1 part dark rum

1 part vodka

½ part curaçao

1 part mango juice

1 part orange juice

1 part pineapple juice

1 part freshly squeezed lime juice

1 cinnamon stick, broken in half

ice cubes

caster sugar, to taste (I generally add 2 tsp per serving)

mint sprigs

1 Shake everything together, except the sugar and mint, over ice cubes in a cocktail shaker, or mix in a jug with lots of ice cubes if you are making a large quantity.

2 Add sugar to taste and stir vigorously until the sugar has dissolved, then add the mint sprigs. Pour into glasses filled with ice cubes to serve.

Allspice

Jamaican people call allspice 'pimento' and it's also known as 'Jamaican pepper' because it has a bit of heat as well as fragrance. Allspice berries come from an elegant tree that grows predominantly in Jamaica. The spice is sold in two forms: ground and as whole berries. Ground allspice is convenient, especially for baking, while the whole berries give you a great flavour, particularly when you pestle-and-mortar them. This works well if you do it with another spice such as black peppercorns as in my Seasoned-up Allspice Chicken with Red Peppers and Coconut (see page 17).

I use allspice in all kinds of cooking, both sweet and savoury – it's great in porridge, marinades, sauces and cakes. The flavour is a three-in-one – nutmeg, clove and cinnamon – plus a bit of black pepper, which is why the Brits in Jamaica first called it 'allspice'. There are just so many flavours in this one little berry.

The famous Jamaican jerk was created from allspice and traditionally involved the whole tree. Jerk cooking began when a hole in the ground filled with pimento wood was used to cook meat that had been seasoned with the berries, then the green pimento leaves were put on top to make it a smoky oven. Every authentic jerk marinade should have allspice in the mix.

Bay Leaves

Everyone should grow a bay tree in their garden or in a container if outside space is limited. It's a versatile herb and the King of Fashion within the pot: a dish with a nice piece of bay leaf sticking out always looks good. I quite often use bay leaves and cinnamon sticks together, in rice dishes and cakes for example, and I use the leaves both fresh and dried. Great in stews, they also have a good flavour when fried. Try them with fruit dishes, too, where their fragrance works beautifully, such as in my Tropical Fruits with Bay, Allspice and Lime Syrup (see page 164).

Cardamom

I got to know cardamom later on in my kitchen life – it didn't feature in the country world where I grew up in Jamaica – but now it's my firm friend. The cardamom pod is very deceptive, packed full of flavours locked up inside, and you'll never know what it possesses until you have undressed it. Once you do that, carefully crushing the hard little seeds within, you'll be amazed how much you want to use them. It's one of those aromas that can go with anything. I've used it in my Coconut and Cardamom Macaroons (see page 146) and it's brilliant in the Honey, Cardamom and Vanilla Fudge (see page 124) as well as my Cardamom and Orange Puddings (see page 155). Its classic partner is coffee, as you'll see from my Coffee and Cardamom Granita with Rum Cream (see page 182).

Cayenne Pepper

The ground seeds of a particular kind of chilli, *Capsicum frutescens*, cayenne has been used in Britain since the 18th century – hot food ain't so new! It's a good way of seasoning meat such as chicken with a dry rub (though for fish I prefer black pepper and Scotch bonnet). You'll find cayenne featured in several of my recipes, including Super-sweet Hot Mash (*see* page 100), Pecan, Parmesan and Cayenne Shortbreads (*see* page 138) and Fried Sweet Potatoes with Cayenne, Coriander and Toasted Coconut (*see* page 97).

Chilli – Fresh

Chilli heat is the most immediate element that turns a bland dish into something that surprises and interests. The King of Flavour is the Scotch bonnet. Once you've bust open a Scotch bonnet, all sorts of things start happening. It's got its own kind of fruitiness that adds a lot of flavour to the dish. And then there's the heat. Your eyes begin watering as soon as you start chopping – it makes you aware of its presence straightaway! The greatest heat is in the seeds, so you can control the power a bit by taking them out, along with the white membrane attaching them to the flesh. But there's always this guess, even once you take the seeds out, as to how hot it's going to be. Scotch bonnets mainly come in three colours: there's a browny-black one I've seen in Jamaica, but green, gold and red is what you get elsewhere. I like to use the green ones in rice and peas or when you are using them whole and don't want them to burst open – this kind has the stronger skin.

Chilli – Dried Chilli Flakes

These are useful to have around in the kitchen to sprinkle into the pot when you haven't got a fresh chilli to hand. I like to use them to flavour my Thyme and Chilli Roasted Tomatoes for serving with pasta (*see* page 80) and in the marinade for BBQ Chicken with Chilli Corn Cakes (*see* page 20).

Cinnamon

This spice is one of my favourites. It's one of the three musketeers along with nutmeg and vanilla, all from the spice island of Grenada, and you often see them sold alongside each other. In summer drinks, hot toddies, homemade juices and punches, these three are good to add on their own or in any combination – but perhaps especially cinnamon. Ground cinnamon is useful for adding to cakes, curries and other savoury dishes, such as my Cuban Hash (*see* page 37), and then cinnamon sticks give a delicious scent to any dish – and they look great, too.

Coriander

This comes in two forms: the fresh leaves and stalks and the seeds. I use the leaves in particular a great deal. It must be the most-loved top tier, giving a vibrant green colour and fresh flavour finish to savoury dishes. The seeds have a lovely, slightly orangey taste that's a valuable addition to many a recipe. Both leaf and seed are used to great effect in my Rum, Chilli and Brown Sugar Cured Salmon (*see* page 48).

Cumin

Cumin seeds often go with coriander seeds in curries and here they both feature in my Indian-style Spiced Pickled Limes (*see* page 152). Aubergines are especially suited to cumin, as you'll see in my Black Bean and Aubergine Stuffed Roasted Peppers (*see* page 104), where cumin is used in its ground form. To get a really rich, fragrant flavour from cumin, toast the seeds in a dry frying pan over a medium heat for a minute or so – take care not to burn them – and then crush them with a pestle and mortar.

Curry Powder

There is a strong Indian element to Caribbean food and curry powder is on every island kitchen shelf. You can make your own using different combinations of spices, or find a good brand. Try it in my Mussel and Sweet Potato Curry (*see* page 56).

Ginger

I love ginger – but that's no surprise, since Jamaica has the best ginger in the world! It's both the particular variety that's cultivated and the soil it's grown in that produce its wonderful taste. Jamaican root ginger isn't as big and beautiful as others – it's smaller and more crackled-looking – but it's got this special fiery flavour that's extra peppery and spicy and goes so well with chilli to create yet more heat. Caribbean curries always have ginger in them. This special spice also has a healthy side and is well known as a detoxing agent. We smash it up, pour on hot water and drink the juice. All Jamaican families grow ginger in their garden and make the root into a drink with demerara sugar and lime.

Ginger appears in every form in this book – ground ginger in cakes, fresh root ginger in curries and savoury dishes, and stem ginger for baking. I also use its sweet syrup in drinks, dressings, cakes and with meat. My Gingered-up Honey and Pear Cake (*see* page 126) is a great pud or tea-time treat, especially with a glass of Dubbed-up Ginger Iced Tea (*see* page 189).

Mint

Mint is a herb I'm really into using. I grew up with its fragrance wafting in through the door from our garden asand we drank it often as a tea. In this book it appears in salads – try my Chicken, Citrus and Pomegranate Salad with Chilli-honey Dressing (*see* page 14) – and other dishes to show what a versatile leaf it is. It's the star of the Cucumber and Mint Salsa that goes with my Chilled Love-apple Soup (*see* page 111). Don't just use it in mint tea – it's really refreshing in cold drinks, too.

Mustard

Ready-made mustard isn't traditionally used in the Caribbean, but as a child the white friends I met through school would take me home to their houses, and this was when I discovered mustard. In this book, I use both grainy mustard, for example in my Mustardy Macaroni Cheese (*see* page 82), and French Dijon mustard. I also like black mustard seeds, which I use when making curries, frying them with a bit of garlic and onion – they look and taste great in the Mango and Coconut Relish (*see* page 166) that's served with my Hot, Hot Roots (*see* page 92).

Nutmeg

So many dishes can do with a fresh grating of nutmeg. Punches and juices come alive with this spice, along with its other two 'partners in crime', vanilla and cinnamon. It nices up anything savoury as well – try my Roasted Nutmeg Cauliflower (*see* page 110), Chicken with Nutmeg, Rum and Bay Leaves (*see* page 16) and Hoppin' Toad-in-the-Hole (*see* page 26). Then there's the sweet stuff, such as the Nutmeg and Rum Cake (*see* page 192), which showcases its power, and it's in plenty of my milky puddings, as well as my special Nutmeg Coconut Custard (*see* page 65). And here's a great Caribbean trick for the cricket pitch: put a whole one in your mouth to keep your mouth moist. Just take care you don't swallow it, or choke – whoops!

Paprika

There are three kinds of paprika that I've used in this book. Hot and sweet paprika are both featured in my Creole Aubergines (*see* page 108), for example, and the smoked variety from Spain turns up on the barbie in the Fire-roasted Artichokes (*see* page 114).

Peppercorns

Black pepper is very Caribbean. Most foods are dry-seasoned with black pepper and salt. It gives you a degree of heat with a completely different taste to Scotch bonnet or dried chilli flakes, with its own quality of warmth and fragrance. In our family café in London, Papine, we mix black pepper and salt together and always have a bowl of it ready for seasoning up fish and for frying (about a 2:1 ratio of black pepper to salt). It's a useful mix to have on hand.

I also like to use green peppercorns, which I crack to release their flavour and put into dishes such as my Steak with Peppercorn and Thyme Sauce (*see* page 34). You can buy peppercorns coarsely ground, or use a pepper grinder. Best of all, pound them with a pestle and mortar to get the freshest of fragrant flavours.

Star Anise

This is a beautiful star-shaped spice that's good in the Chinese-influenced dishes that are so common in the Caribbean. In this book you can try it in the Soy, Chilli and Star Anise Spiced Mackerel Fillets (*see* page 44).

Tamarind

Tamarind is a fruit that I used to scrump as a child. We'd sneak into gardens and go get it. I even used to enjoy it green – young boys love baby green tamarind – though it could give you a bit of a stomachache, as you're only really meant to eat tamarind when it's brown and ripe. Most people in Jamaica think of tamarind as tamarind balls – the paste around a seed coated with sugar, like a natural sweet that you suck right down to the seed.

Tamarind is very sour and cooks use it as a souring agent. You get it in liquid form or in a block, which you chop up and soak, then use the liquid. I like the ready-to-use liquid tamarind because you can add it directly to your cooking pot. Try it with lamb in my Hot Chops with an Orange and Tamarind Glaze (*see* page 32).

Thyme

This is such a useful herb. It's one that anyone can grow, in the garden or in a pot or window box – it's so satisfying to use something you've raised with your own hand. Jamaicans use a lot of thyme. You can break off a handful and chuck it in a pot of soup or stew and let it cook away. Once the leaves have fallen off, you can take out the stems before or after serving. You can also flake off the leaves first, chop them up and use them in sauces or as a meat seasoning, such as in my Spicy Scotch Eggs (*see* page 62). In my kitchen it's mostly chopped up, leaves, stems and everything, and chucked in to get the most from its nice, fresh, outdoors flavour.

Dried thyme is also useful and has a much better flavour than most dried herbs. Thyme can even be used in sweet foods – just try my Orange, Thyme and Curaçao Ice Cream (*see* page 154).

Vanilla

I never saw a vanilla pod until I came to the UK – in Jamaica it was always the extract. I grew up seeing my grandmother use vanilla extract and it's great to have to hand. But now the whole pod has become a favourite ingredient of mine because it looks so beautiful, and the visual part of food is important.

Vanilla goes well with many other flavours and one of the classic combinations is with chocolate, so it's in my Wicked Caribbean Hot Chocolate (*see* page 132) and my White Chocolate and Vanilla Mousse (*see* page 130). But you may be surprised to learn that it works in savoury dishes, too – as in my Pork Chops with Coconut and Vanilla (*see* page 29).

ACKNOWLEDGEMENTS

I'd like to thank Hattie Ellis, Diana Henry, Sara Lewis, Sarah O'Keefe, Chris Terry, photographic assistants Danny and Steve, Borra Garson, Emma Hughes, Charlene Davies, all the crew at Mitchell Beazley, and all my family.

One love,
Levi Roots

I dedicate this book to my grandmother Miriam Small and my mother Doreen Graham — they really are the source (sauce) of all my inspiration.

Spice it up!
LEVI ROOTS

First published in Great Britain in 2011 by Mitchell Beazley, an imprint of Octopus Publishing Group Limited, Endeavour House, 189 Shaftesbury Avenue, London, WC2H 8JY.
www.octopusbooks.co.uk

An Hachette UK Company
www.hachette.co.uk

ISBN: 978 1 84533 592 2

A CIP record for this book is available from the British Library.

Set in American Typewriter. Grotesque, and Pene.

Printed and bound in China.

Consultants | Hattie Ellis and Diana Henry
Commissioning Editor | Becca Spry
Senior Editor | Leanne Bryan
Art Director and Designer | Pene Parker
Copy Editor | Jo Richardson
Photographer | Chris Terry
Home Economist | Sara Lewis
Stylist | Sarah O'Keefe
Proofreader | Abi Waters
Indexer | Helen Snaith
Senior Production Controller | Lucy Carter